CARL BARÂT

Threepenny Memoir

The Lives of a Libertine

FOURTH ESTATE • *London*

First published in Great Britain in 2010 by
Fourth Estate
An imprint of HarperCollins*Publishers*
77–85 Fulham Palace Road
London W6 8JB
www.4thestate.co.uk

Visit our authors' blog: www.fifthestate.co.uk

A catalogue record for this book is available from the British Library

ISBN 978-0-00-739376-3

Typeset in 11.25/20pt Minion by Palimpsest Book Production Limited,
Falkirk, Stirlingshire

Printed in Great Britain by Clays Ltd, St Ives plc

CONTENTS

ONE

Raising the Colours

The room looked like the cover of the *Sgt. Pepper* album come to life: the great and the good, the infamous, the notorious and the inane all gathered under an opulent domed roof, lit up in blushes of colour, celebrating another year for the NME Awards. A dense bass guitar made the soles of my feet tingle as the room rubbernecked at a Stetson that was cutting a determined swathe towards the plush, red stairs Peter and I were standing on. Diminutive, and lit like she had her own spotlight, the lady beneath the cowboy hat tilted high on her head gave us a winning smile, before leaning towards us.

'Hello, The Strokes,' she purred warmly before disappearing towards the door behind us.

It was our first ever NME Awards ceremony and Madonna had just confirmed that it wasn't our year.

* * *

Looking back at The Libertines is like catching flashes of sunlight between buildings as you race by on a train. An old film reel where the spools are weathered and worn, leaving empty frames on the screen. Faces disappear and reappear, sights crackle and fade as we aimlessly walk the streets of an ever-changing London, pub-crawling, minesweeping – secretly topping up our drinks from half-full glasses left unattended by their owners. We dream of Albion and the high skies above the low ceiling of our basement flat.

Sometimes there's no noise and sometimes that's all there is.

It's 2003 and we're about to go on stage. Gary and John are warming up, I can hear the thrum of the bass, the ricochet of the snare. Peter takes my hand and, barely acknowledging the rest of the band: 'Just you and me, we can do this without them. You have to believe.' He's almost in tears as he says it. Gary and John find something to stare at on the floor. My stomach turns over. Peter starts in again: 'Something's going to happen tonight', and I envisage some sort of imminent meltdown on stage. It's the equivalent of your girlfriend telling you that she needs a serious talk with you that evening: you know it's never going to be good news. Then, nothing happens. Peter plays a storming set; he's all over the stage, heralding the crowd, grinning at us three. Bumping chests, we collide at the centre of the stage, and to an onlooker it would seem like there was nowhere else we'd rather be.

When we were performing, I used to worry about being found out, that I didn't deserve to be on that stage. I'd swap glances with John and Gary and we'd get on with it, we'd buckle down as we always did. But then there was this other part of me that knew how lucky we were, that knew we gelled, and how lucky we were that, without trying, me and Peter had a chemistry; we fitted together completely – which made it all the more difficult when he tried to wrench it all apart. I can see those lights, feel the sweat gather at the small of my back. I've never been happier, I've never been more angry, never more fulfilled or let down. The Libertines heightened my insecurities, made me feel like I was king of the world, realized my dreams and dashed my hopes. We were that kind of band.

* * *

Before The Libertines, before the madness and the money, before the room started filling up with people we didn't know, Peter and I would romanticize about Albion. I don't even know when we first started saying it. It was something that, many years ago, Peter and I, if we were trying to motivate the other to do something, we'd say: 'Do it for the Albion', and it would work. It would spur us into action even if it did sound as if we were talking about West Brom. Most people wouldn't even have bothered to dress it up: they'd just have told you they had goals, but we imagined ourselves on a voyage sailing through choppy waters, on a ship called the *Albion* looking for Arcadia. That might sound vaguely nonsensical or highfalutin to other people, but as far as I'm concerned that's the voyage I'm on. If you are going to set sail, then you have to give your vessel a name, and my good ship's called the *Albion*. For the sake of home and hope and glory, let's sail to Arcadia, an unfettered place with no constraints and infinite hope. That's the destination. We held Albion and Arcadia close, twisted it into our own philosophy; we changed and mutated it along the way. It was our own personal mythology, our idiosyncratic, romantic ideal. It was the Greek myths with England at their heart: Homer and Blake.

The whole idea of Albion has got tangled up over the years, but the important thing was that Peter and I met in the middle with it; we chimed with that ideal. I truly believe that we're still on that boat – at the very opposite ends of it right now, but still stuck on the same fucking sea.

* * *

I've lived in London since the summer of 1996, when I moved up to study drama at Brunel University. I wasn't particularly popular in Whitchurch, near Basingstoke, where I grew up. I was something of a ghost, felt straitjacketed there, and had to move away. Some people pick their point of the compass and stick to it; all I ever wanted to be was at the heart of the action.

Richmond, though, seemed very far from that. It's where I lived for most of my two short years at Brunel, hunkered down in the student halls on campus. I met Peter there, which was important in itself, but campus life also allowed me to plug into London's social scene and student life meant I had money in my pocket – a ludicrous notion for most students now – as well as all the time in the world to spend it. I was always annoyed that my Richmond halls didn't have a London postcode – they were in TW1, on the other side of the river – so I ended up moving with a friend to Sheen, in the first of many moves towards the heart of London. Sheen was SW14, I think, and we had a little old house next to Richmond Park, into which we used to creep at night and steal wood to burn in our fireplace, ambling back through the darkness weighed down with piles of wood. We'd cycle into Richmond together on my bike, the two of us careering along, one of us on the crossbar like the scene from *Butch Cassidy and the Sundance Kid*, 'Raindrops Keep Fallin' On My Head' running through my head, going way too fast, two miles there and two miles back. We thrived on the bright lights of central London, and every trip home from town was spent on the number 9 bus, which would inevitably see us waking up in Kingston, the end of the line, bodies contorted and mouths drooling, faces pressed up against the glass, Richmond some miles back. Kingston's a very unforgiving place at seven in the morning. The driver would never let us stay on board the bus, even though there were never any other buses there and it would always be the next to depart. We'd stand for twenty minutes, bleary-eyed in the freezing cold, until he allowed us back on for the return journey – at which point we'd fall asleep again and wake up in fucking town. Sometimes it felt endless.

Peter's sister Amy-Jo Doherty was the only person at Brunel I really felt a connection with during my short time studying there. From my vantage point in Whitchurch I'd imagined that, when going to London to university, I'd take rooms, and there'd be a succession of characters who'd process through my digs wearing bottle-green tweeds and carrying armfuls of leather-bound books tied with packing string – I think in my head I was going to Oxford circa 1930 in an Evelyn Waugh novel. What I actually found were people with golf clubs and *Best of 1994* dance CDs. Amy-Jo was the one person I met there who seemed engaged with the sort of things I was looking for. We became best friends and she'd often tell me fantastic stories about Peter, an aspiring poet who was a year younger than her and still lived in the sticks. When he finally came up to visit, she asked me to look after him while she went to an evening class. He wasn't really as I expected: very tall and wearing a kind of plastic jacket, looking quite 'street' – but then he's always courageous with his outfits. The family resemblance was more than incredible. I'd heard a lot of good things about him, and he was interested in me because his big sister used to come home and talk about the new world of university, and particularly about this friend she'd met.

Straight away we began to talk about music. He was a massive Morrissey and Smiths fan, and his sister had asked me to write down the tablature to 'This Charming Man', but I didn't know anything about The Smiths, and I'd transcribed 'Charmless Man' by Blur, instead. He didn't play guitar very well, so I showed him a few things, and he played me his one song, 'The Long Song', which lived up to its name. I had some songs with terrible lyrics, and we started doing musical things together; we bonded over music very quickly. That first night, too, we had an argument over the meaning of a word. I can't even remember what the word was now, but, finally, it felt as if I was getting the intellectual stimulation I'd been searching for and had been expecting from university. For me, it was a joyful moment.

We began to meet up every time he came to town. He lived and breathed London – he'd go to charity shops and buy massive shoes and corduroy trousers, kitsch tea sets and Chris Barber vinyls, and he had a certificate to show he'd climbed the Monument – and just loved to draw it all in, for all the right reasons. I found that very charming. I was learning things from him, too, although I wouldn't have readily admitted it. I was performing the role of the older, experienced guy, and I'd try to play it like he was the little'un nipping at my feet. But in reality Peter knew a lot about the world I wanted to know. He'd read and read, and searched for authors to inspire him, and, by helping this passion come alive in me, helped me become more the person I wanted to be. He only made the trip to London every once in a while, so things progressed slowly. We'd said from the very beginning that we wanted to start a band, and kept on repeating it but to little effect. Amy would get him on the phone when we were out at night, drunk, and he'd say, 'What about this band, then?' That was all it was for a while – good intentions and drunken promises. It must have been a couple of years after we first met that we finally sat down properly, at my house. We wrote a song that became 'The Good Old Days' that first night, along with quite a few others, and I remember us sitting there, staring at each other in silence as the clock ticked towards dawn, searching for the right words. We were trying to find a line for the middle eight, and he'd tell you differently but I'm absolutely sure it was me who came up with it. Finally, we had: 'A list of things we said we'd do tomorrow.' We've argued since about whose line it was, but that seemed to be a moment when everything slotted into place, and it was quite a forerunner of things to come.

*   *   *

London, its streets and neighbourhoods, litter my lyrics, and I can always find some part of it to suit my mood. I first felt plugged in to the city at a place called the Foundry on Old Street. They're knocking it down now to build a grand hotel or something, to cash in on the area's cool – Shoreditch surgically removing its own heart – but Peter used to run a night there called Arcadia, a performance poetry thing, which he used to revel in. I'd come along and play the piano very badly, but it was art so the quality of the performance didn't really matter. We'd get free Guinness and we'd host a raffle to make money. I think the most auspicious prize we gave away was half a gram of speed and a Charles Manson record, but it always made us a couple of bob for a few beers and a fine breakfast.

London really began for me, though, in Camden and Soho. I have such a strong image of Camden from those days, entrancing but horrific, edgy and dark and hilarious, at least partly thanks to some of the characters who made up the Camden contingent. Irish Paul was in a band called The Samaritans and was the kind of legend that my Camden was made of. He was part of our schooling, older than us, as was Essex Tom and another guy called Max. They were the big boys, the older brothers, and when they spoke you pricked up your ears and listened. I was always a bit cautious around them, though, as they'd drink, fuck and fight whoever or whatever they could find. We'd be walking down the street and Max would have this really demonic look in his eye, then pause, apologize, and leg it up Parkway to knock seven bells out of a couple of students who were being lairy and drunk. Then he'd come back again and resume the conversation as if nothing had happened. Essex Tom I remember from his run-in with John Hassall's girlfriend, a girl called Jenny who'd had a boob job and therefore instantly became known as Jenny with the Big Knackers on Holloway Road. It wasn't always poetry and lofty ideals with The Libertines. Anyway, one day we were all sat around in a pub and Tom took John's camera from the table and went to the toilets to film his dick – a dick, moreover, with a notorious kink in it. John took the camera home without realizing and, later, Jenny with the Big Knackers on Holloway Road stumbled across it and recognized Tom from the footage. I think her relationship with John was doomed from thereon in.

Irish Paul, on the other hand, had a Dickensian air about him, and I remember when he invited all of his mates to a celebratory dinner one night at the Mango Room in Camden just after it had opened. 'My ship's come in,' he told the assembled company. 'You've stuck with me through the lean times, each sorted me out when I've needed it, so now it's your turn. I'm going to treat you all to a night out. Tuck in, fill your boots.'

I felt touched, a real part of his gang, the inner circle, and we had a great evening. Then, at the end of an incredible meal, just as the bill was presented, Irish Paul got up: 'I hope you've got your running shoes on, you boys,' he said, then he ran straight out of the restaurant and away down the street into the night. There was a significant pause and then all hell broke loose as we all bolted for the door. It was like the rush to get on the last helicopter out of Saigon.

There was another Paul, Rock Paul, an American, who'd been

a fixture at the Good Mixer through all the different crowds and bands who came and went. He just sat up at the bar, watched them come and watched them go, and drank. One night, we were all in there, about to embark on a session, and Rock Paul walked in looking utterly stricken. 'I've had some really bad news,' he said, and it fell very quiet, the only noise the clicking of balls on the pool table behind us. 'I'm terminally ill with cancer.' We were shattered. All I could think about was an empty stool, another face fading from the scene, and the Mixer, Camden, London, everywhere being the poorer for it. It got very sad, and slow, and we started to exchange stories, buy drinks for the fellow, reminisce about the good times we'd had and the good times we'd dedicate to his memory when he'd gone. At the end of the night, we were all mellow and drunk, giving hugs and saying goodbyes, and Rock Paul, on his way out, admitted he'd made the whole thing up. That he just wanted us to buy drinks for him. We were horrified and dumbfounded, but slightly in awe that he'd play the cancer card just to get free drinks. Passing him in the doorway, Welsh Paul gave him a level look that suggested he'd best not try that again, but I think that even he admired the gall of it. Cancer in exchange for a few drinks: how do you meter that out?

* * *

That was the Camden that made us, formed The Libertines, but the centre of my world, the heart of Albion, was undoubtedly Waterloo. It was where the city first came into sharp relief for me when I was fifteen, where, with a few friends, I came blinking into the light as we descended from the train for the first time. We were country bumpkins at their most inoffensive and wide-eyed, innocence personified in Jim Morrison T-shirts and old German army boots. It felt like the whole world was watching us as we slunk into dodgy bars in Soho, tentatively asking for that first drink then suddenly cocksure when they served us. We trawled the illegal twenty-four-hour joints along the back of Archer Street and felt as if we were in a film, though the magic waned briefly for me when I walked into a toilet and saw someone jacking up as he leant against a tiled wall. I was equally freaked out and awed. From a distance, London had always been faded glamour and drinking underage; coming face to face with hard drugs in a sleazy bar was all I could have hoped for, a ridiculous notion that really does lend weight to the phrase 'Be careful what you wish for'. At fifteen the rush was almost physical. The three of us then went to a peep show in Soho with about three quid between us, and squeezed into a single booth, the smell of cleaning fluid making our noses wrinkle and our eyes red. Then, as our tingling anticipation built, the screen slid up to reveal an empty room with an old bike propped up against the wall. The emptiness was almost a relief . . . and then something moved in the corner, a woman you could best describe as tatty, reading a paperback, with part of Spider-Man tattooed across her face. She stood up, her book still hanging from one hand, and gyrated momentarily before us. Then the screen came down, and I think we were all secretly pleased it did. Strangely, I was glad the moment wasn't sexy. My dream of London was of decaying beauty and a brittle, tawdry sheen of glamour. I had wanted to see the workings beneath the surface and that afternoon in Soho they couldn't have been more visible.

* * *

After I dropped out of Brunel and Peter came to town, we set sail together around London, moving from squat to flat, to mates' houses and then back again. Peter found the first important place: DeLaney Mansions, 360 Camden Road. Our landlord was just like Del Boy, had Del Boy been Greek and fond of shell suits and gaudy chains heavy enough to sink him if he fell in the Thames. It was a sixties bedsit that time forgot. The front door didn't work, so we had to exit and enter via the window, which we half-heartedly secured with a bicycle chain. Not that we had anything worth stealing. We had so little, in fact, that we shared a mattress on the floor and a kitchenette, and that was it. We had two cyberpunks for upstairs neighbours, a couple who looked like characters from a William Gibson novel: plastic straws in their hair, huge shoes, multiple unappealing piercings. They practically lived on speed. He was a computer programmer (ironic, given that he looked like he belonged in *Tron*) from Philadelphia; she was an Israeli, quite mad, and with a rather strange sideline. People would pay her cash to go into their houses and beat them up, which I found both creepy and enterprising. The cyberpunks would clomp around above our heads all day, but if we made the slightest sound on our acoustic guitars they'd start screaming and banging the floor. One night a brick came through the window. We looked out through the jagged hole and it was the Israeli, screaming in at us, shouting, 'Fuck you!'

We called the police, the first and only time we ever called them, I think. But nothing much could be done about it and the upshot was that we had a broken window for the next four months. It was winter, naturally.

We then moved along Camden Road to number 236, where Peter sweet-talked a family who had bought a big house there who we helped move in. The house was a mix of old bedsits and small flats and sat atop a huge basement. The basement was a real mess, but you could see the potential in it, and they gave it to us to live in while they made the place into a home. So we had this glorious subterranean Victorian expanse with a garden, and a grand old toilet cistern; it reminded me of ringing a church bell every time I pulled the heavy chain to flush it. That was where we began to forge our legend, where we started throwing impromptu gigs and parties. We'd flyer Camden and invite people back there and play for them, revelling in the randomness and the unexpected that this brought. At the first ever gig there, we'd decorated the place with lots of candles, and Peter had been to visit his parents in Germany and come back with lots of beer and cigarettes, which we'd put out for people. Everyone sat expectantly around, waiting for us to begin and, as soon as we played the first chord, all the lights went out. We had to ask around for a pound for the meter, but got things going again eventually and it turned into a very long, debauched party. Irish Paul shagged someone in the bathroom, which at the time we thought was particularly impressive, and that first night created the template for all the gigs there to come. The locust swarm would descend, we'd play, and they'd leave us, sometimes days later, with only debris and hazy recollections to show for it. The flat would be wrecked, but we'd be happy. Later, after we were signed, the so-called 'guerrilla' gigs would take over the mantle. They came about because, by that time, the internet was becoming a force in everyone's lives, and we were knocked sideways by the way you could post 'Gig tomorrow night' on a forum somewhere and, as if by magic, people would turn up. The guerrilla gigs were chaotic and disorganized because there was no time to sort anything out, and precious little money, too, but the fact that people would turn up was a real buzz. They were a continuation of the impromptu gigs at 236 Camden Road, in the same *mi casa es su casa* spirit. They were about anyone being able to reach out and touch the people in the pictures on their wall, the musicians they were listening to at the time, about pushing all the boundaries, seeing how far that was possible. It was the best fun imaginable, and everyone was invited.

Remarkably, the family upstairs at 236 Camden Road looked on us as some kind of novelty. They never batted an eyelid even when we serenaded up to seventy people at a time below them. Then we hit upon the idea of sub-letting the space under the stairwell to a French conceptual artist who we charged twenty pounds a week. He was happy there in our basement. And so was I, for a while.

I was always much happier on Camden Road than I was later, living on the top floor of a townhouse in Holloway, which, looking back, was an exercise in making myself feel edgy. Some nights I even slept in a cage, in the spare room of a prostitute we'd made friends with, a woman we'll call Natasha. Natasha worked from home, I suppose you could say; she ran it as a sort of brothel and, when she wasn't working, she hung around Camden a lot, a face at our shows. Someone said she knew one of the guys in Blur, but I don't know. What I do know was we needed somewhere to sleep, and she had the space, so we took her up on her offer, despite its pitfalls. Natasha looked like a beautiful fourteen-year-old boy: skinny, emaciated and striking, and she was an enigma. She thought it would age her being outside too long, took cabs everywhere, and wouldn't leave the house without applying sun block – a very paranoid girl, and quite lonely as far as I could tell. The bedroom I was allocated had a big iron cage in it, halfway between an outsize birdcage and a medieval torture device, which I often ended up sleeping in. I think her clients used to spend their hours in there paying to suffer, but it afforded me a degree of security I enjoyed. Natasha was our drummer for a few hours; we liked the notion, but she really couldn't drum.

When she had a client, Peter and I would sit in the next room holding pellet guns and talk in gruff voices so that, through the wall, one might think that she had muscle to look after her in case a client freaked out. As a thank-you she'd usually take us to the café across the road and feed us, which seemed a fair exchange. Peter and I used to spy on her and her clients, sometimes, crawling quietly around on our knees to peep through the keyhole. I remember seeing her with a Hassidic Jew and, surprisingly, the drummer from a band we knew. Not at the same time, of course. We sat back dumbfounded when we caught sight of him on the other side of the door.

However, the boarding arrangement couldn't, and didn't, last. A few months in, Peter found a new girlfriend, which Natasha didn't like at all. She could be quite possessive and paranoid, and she used to have these fits and attacks that she seemed totally convinced by, but which we never quite fully believed in. We used to take her to hospital and she'd always rally and make a recovery, a little miracle every time. She claimed to be able to see auras around people, and know high-ups in government, clients, she said, who were in positions of terrible power. One night she left a note to say goodbye and perched out on the window ledge feigning a suicide attempt. There was another suicide note pinned on the door one day when we got back from somewhere, and we ran into the kitchen where she had her head in the electric oven. I'm not sure she enjoyed the sound of our laughter, and I don't think we were laughing because we thought the situation funny. Fundamentally, we were pretty scared of her. In the end I took the coward's way out and fled to Manchester in the middle of the night. Peter had already gone, and I was getting the fear alone in my cage. Someone told me Natasha has since moved to Ireland, but if ever I'm on the Holloway Road I still tread lightly.

* * *

They were lazy days on the whole, though, and when there was no wind to fill our sails Peter and I would drift in slow circles, becalmed, waiting for the currents to bear us away. After we left Holloway, we moved to Dalston, where Peter had a room and I was sort of squatting. Also there was Don, whose place it was, who was eccentric at best, and another guy, Mad Mick, who lived up to his name and was always hanging around. Nothing much moved on those long hot days, cars hummed in and out of sight, and we lay listlessly in sunlit windows trying to feel the world turn. Downstairs there were a couple of French girls who spent their spare time attempting to make ketamine out of rose-water that they'd bought at the chemist. They'd spend afternoons boiling all sorts of ingredients in rose-water, because one night at a club someone had given them a bum tip that that was how you made the stuff, but they were having about as much luck with that as most alchemists have conjuring up gold. Mad Mick was from Brooklyn, and I liked him. He was quiet and self-contained, but a lunatic with it, and it was as if he lived in the shadows: you'd only see him at very strange times, like six in the morning at Dalston Kingsland train station when he really lived over in Kentish Town. We'd always meet him at the most odd, out-of-the-way places with the oddest people. We'd show up at a random squat party in Deptford and he'd be there. I was in a Jobcentre in Hackney once in an interminable wait to see someone and I suggested we start breakdancing and, without another word, he did. He was a damn good breakdancer, and it made the surly staff feel uncomfortable, which was a bonus.

During those early days we got a gig in a nursing home in East Ham because our drummer at the time knew one of the nurses there and we'd been promised £50 if we did this gig for the old people. So we trooped down and were confronted by a room of very fragile and vulnerable old people, the kind of old people, shockingly old, you don't see on the street any more because they can't really get around. I feel quite bad about it now. About the most suitable song in our repertoire was a cover of 'Anything But Love', the old jazz standard, and we tried to be quiet, but we weren't especially good at that, and there were a lot of fingers in ears and a lot of confusion. People kept getting up and walking around, as if they weren't quite sure what was going on, or where the door was. One of the patients there was called Margie, and she took rather a shine to us; the poor lady had alcoholic dementia and kept asking if we'd brought a pint with us. We persisted, though, and by the end of our set a few people seemed into it. Then a couple of nurses came in and quietly drew a curtain around one of the beds. It transpired that its occupant had died during our performance of 'Music When The Lights Go Out'. It was a pretty incomprehensible moment for us, but the nurses took it entirely in their stride. It might sound cold, but I suppose that's just how it is in a hospice. It was terribly tragic, but what a pertinent song to go out on. There are, I imagine, worse ways to go.

To add to the surreal turn that the day had taken, before the gig we'd told Mad Mick that he could be our manager. We didn't really want him to be, and of course there wasn't a job because we didn't really need a manager back then, but it was just a cool thing to tell people none the less. We'd said to Mick that if he ran to the gig from Dalston then the job was his. As we left the hospice after this terrible confusion, just as we were driving off, we saw Mick at the end of the road, huffing and puffing. He had just arrived, had run all the way, but there wasn't room in the car to give him a lift back so we had to leave him there. I remember looking in the rear-view mirror and there was Mad Mick, confused and red-faced, sweating in his jeans, getting smaller and smaller until he was only a speck.

Gigs like that were clearly not going to pay, so I had a series of other, mostly crap, jobs that I sometimes enjoyed but mostly resented. Waterloo had been my gateway to the world, but the altogether less lovely Hammersmith was my gateway to the world of work. The temp agency there saw something in me that I'm not all too sure I saw in myself, dispatching me across London to push paper around like a clerk in the background in an Ealing comedy. For a while, I was at the BBC, and I looked out over west London from my office at Television Centre, a network of endless corridors and boxy rooms that held about as much charm as pleurisy. I was twenty-one, and an easily distracted employee at best. The wages were criminal and, feeling hard done by, I spent my days roaming the corridors wearing a suit and a trilby, which wasn't really done back then, and flirting with random BBC employees, ambitious girls who really didn't care if I lived or died, though the hat piqued their interest. I was a purchase ledger clerk, which mean paying the BBC employees, though I can't quite remember ever paying anyone or not. At the same time, I was performing in the house band at a place called Jazz After Dark on Greek Street in Soho. The four of us played for four hours a night for the princely sum of £20 (between us, not each) and a bottle of beer apiece. Which, considering that none of us could actually play jazz, was probably fair enough. My undoing was oversleeping one morning after a gig and missing my shift. The BBC drafted in another temp to do my job, a temp who accomplished, I was reliably informed, my whole eight hours' work in the first five minutes of the day. It was fair to say that they were on to me.

After that, I worked at Cobb's Hall in Hammersmith, which wasn't a place for a suit or trilby. I was on the front desk, or the front line as I came to think of it, for a building full of social workers. A lot of their clients were mental health patients, a good portion of them schizophrenics, who came in to get their injections to offset their psychosis. I won't pretend to understand what went on in the clinic or what disorders some of the people were struggling with, but I was pretty much the first face they saw when they came in. So I had people who were overdue their injections, very interesting people, very angry people, some telling me they're the Son of God and they need to kill me, and there's no security. Just me sitting there in splendid isolation. I had a little black alarm cord that, when you pulled it, made a sound that I can only describe as inoffensive, and that was my only protection. All for £5 an hour. I never got hurt, although came close to it, but there was an impreciseness to their plans, so when they loomed up it wasn't too difficult to get out of the way. In quieter moments I used to go through the computer system and see who was on file. I found a few people I knew.

Far more pleasant were the three years I spent off and on as an usher in London's theatres. The job excited me if only because it let me in on the periphery of the glittering world I'd imagined London to be. I was still outside its walls, but I could finally see in at the windows. Before I moved to London, I'd get home from a day trip to the West End, turn on the TV and there was the city again, and it seemed fantastic to me that I'd been somewhere that was on the box, that it actually existed. When I moved there, I'd go back to places again and again, and remember standing in the cobbled square in Covent Garden early one morning with a light mist on the streets and no one around. I fancied I heard the flower market starting up across the way, blooms brought on trestle tables. I imagined Oscar Wilde, the comings and goings of *My Fair Lady*, I romanticized it out of all proportion and it took me a long time to realize that it was a modern-day tourist trap. When I was working at the theatres I used to go down to the Piazza in my lunch hours and watch the performers, and I'd see people in sleeping bags waiting to perform for the tourists and people a little too drunk for lunchtime, and I realized that the only place that the romantic Covent Garden lived on in was in the hearts of people like me. And, little by little, the lustre faded. The world inside the theatre, however, still held some magic, and I particularly liked working at the Old Vic. It was near my spiritual home of Waterloo – the portal to this new world for a country boy like me – and I loved its tradition and its history; it signified something and felt real to me. I had one pair of blue trousers and a horrible matching waistcoat that I wore for all my theatre work; the trousers were a pair of flares that were so worn that they shone. They never got washed because I had nowhere to wash them, and at one point I had impetigo on my legs that I couldn't help rubbing, and the trousers eventually blended with the scab. But those trousers carried me through, from my initial days among shadowy aisles pointing patrons to their seats to the day our Rough Trade deal finally allowed me to fold them neatly along their thinning creases and put them away for good.

That might make everything sound very purposeful, but the truth was that I didn't have any sense of where we were going while I was at the Old Vic, though Peter and I were increasingly inseparable and working more and more intensely on our lyrics. Peter was always very optimistic but somehow – and this is probably indicative of the insecurities that would dog me all the way through my performing career – I never thought I'd make it in a band. For me, it was an impenetrable world, and playing in front of a small audience was already intimidating enough. Peter's attitude was different: *We can do this, you can be that.* He was full of faith, life and vitality, and that sustained me; it was a real part of the magic of the time. Peter surprised me at work at the Old Vic one night, when we were meant to be rehearsing but I'd taken the paying job instead. Separate worlds – music and theatre – colliding momentarily, almost causing one to spin helplessly out of orbit. I was in my trusty trousers, probably gleaming in the theatre lights, serving a platter of vol-au-vents as part of a reception for Marcel Marceau. It was an after-show as far as I can remember – as much as great mime artists have after-shows, anyway. Then Peter just appeared, lumbering into sight, red-faced with tears in his eyes. I can't imagine what the guests must have thought as a stranger button-holed one of the waiters, and the quiet of the theatre bar is shattered as he screams: 'What are you doing here? Can't you see these people are cunts? We're meant to be writing songs!'

The room screeched to a halt, a hundred heads turning towards us, now centre stage in the encroaching silence. I was livid. How I kept my job there is still a mystery.

As well as the Old Vic, I did stints at the Aldwych, the Apollo and the Lyric. Ushering is a funny job, mostly populated by hopeful actors and musicians, a lot of whom fall by the wayside and get stuck in that routine. The idea is that it'll subsidize your earnings and allow you to pursue your dreams during the daylight hours, but the reality is that you all end up going to the same cliquey bars after the show, spend all your money and then sleep all day. Many people get stuck in that for years. It wasn't entirely without merit: I got to meet Harold Pinter and Michael Gambon, an impressive man who seemed to have a glow about him. I even had a chance to speak with him too, and he gave me some advice.

'What is your purpose?' he asked.

I mumbled something about going to drama school, breaking into acting – I was still very young and shy – and he looked me directly in the eye and said: 'Don't worry about that bullshit, just lie. I got an agent on the strength of saying I did this thing at the Old Vic and it was a total lie.' He was quite encouraging, and pleasingly unprincipled, too, as far as I could tell.

* * *

For a short while we called the band The Strand, principally because, during my breaks as an usher at the Aldwych Theatre I used to walk up and down the Strand wondering when it was I would be randomly offered a part in a film or even to be scouted to be a model. Those were the kind of dumb things I'd sometimes do. London for me back then was limitless, and I was naïve and silly. I just assumed that there was a chance anyone could make it, get lucky. Funnily enough, it never happened like that, but the band name stuck for a period, one of our many awful names, along with The Cricketers and The Sallys. Then I suggested The Libertines: we'd had a well-thumbed copy of the Marquis de Sade's *Lusts of the Libertines* floating around the band for as long as I could remember. That name was, briefly, rejected, though I can't imagine why: none of us was particularly enamoured with the idea of being called The Sallys or The Strand.

Later, by utter coincidence, we found out that the Sex Pistols used to be called The Strand. I met Glenn Matlock backstage when we supported them at Crystal Palace and the only conversation I could think of, while he's sitting there drinking herbal tea and I was drunk and looking for drugs, was to tell him that my band used to be called The Strand, too. It must have sounded like a complete lie, the sort of thing you'd make up just to cosy up to him, to let him know that you really knew all about the Pistols. I felt a ridiculous need to make conversation because I was a fan, and really wanted to talk to the Sex Pistols. He, meanwhile, simply regarded me quietly over his tea. It was at a football stadium, and so we were standing in our dressing room, trying not to worry too much and just enjoy it, and the Pistols were in the room next door. I could hear John Lydon saying, and I think he was talking about Keith Flint, 'I was doing that, I had that haircut twenty years ago, cheeky sod.' That made us roll about with laughter, deliriously happy just to be a part of it, to be that close to the inner circle.

Even though we were playing in front of all the Sex Pistols' gear, the stage was a vast expanse. It was a magnificent day, perfect for a festival, and the crowd was made up of families and lots of blokes in their late thirties and forties, out for the day reliving their youth. Punk pomp with pushchairs. We had our matching red army jackets on in the blisteringly hot sun, and we tried to get them going, but they all started to sing 'Yellow Submarine' at us, I think on account of our jackets. That just fired us up, so we ripped off our tunics to expose skinny bare flesh, this pasty punk flesh, which for reasons I've yet to fathom always goes down a treat. Suddenly they seemed to be on our side. Fear and adrenalin meant that we were going mental, fucking giving it as hard as we could and we really, really meant it. I think that came across, and our enthusiasm was reciprocated by a very partisan audience. They were there for one band and we weren't that band. Later on I remember reading Steven Wells' review of the gig and I think we got a quick mention, which I was pleased about. The Sex Pistols are a pretty hard band to support.

Afterwards, I bumped into John Lydon and I asked if he'd seen the show. 'Libertines!' he said.

'Yes,' I replied.

'I don't miss a trick,' he said and shot off.

We were pretty much ordered to go to the after-show party. I remember someone who might have been Lydon's minder pointing his finger at us and shouting at us to do so. I'm assuming that John Lydon's quite into drum and bass, because the party was at a rough drum and bass place in Wandsworth High Street, which I found a bit odd. Peter took a chair from the Lydon group, and he's a massive Lydon fan so he was crestfallen when Lydon said to him, 'Hey, what are you doing? Those chairs are for us; they're our chairs. Be fair!'

The drink and fervour of the day had taken their hold when I started asking Lydon if he could get us any drugs. 'I'm not your drug dealer,' he said, 'but I shall speak to the proprietor and see what I can do.' Looking back, I doubt he did, and I must have asked him another four times that night before he took our manager to one side and said, 'I am not his drug dealer.' I stopped asking him after that. At least I hope I did.

* * *

I think if you'd said to us back when we lived on the Camden Road that only a couple of years hence, just a hop over the millennium, we'd be supporting the Sex Pistols, I would have laughed you out of town. On millennium eve, I was with Johnny Borrell and his girlfriend, Jen, and we were drunk. We'd left it too late to organize our evening, we couldn't get near any of the celebrations so – and I'm still not sure how we hit on the idea – we went down to the Kingsway underpass knowing that it led directly to Waterloo Bridge. The crowds were milling about as we disappeared into the gaping darkness and clambered over the locked gate. We stumbled along, for about half a mile, the sound of London fading behind us, until we came out right in the heart of the celebrations, the Thames below us, the sky full of gassy sulphur. It was exhilarating, euphoric. We walked into the middle of it all with a bottle of Cava. Everyone had been wondering for years where they were going to be in 2000, and I was in the epicentre of my universe: Waterloo.

That moment seemed freighted with significance, seemed to be one of the rare times I was in the right place at the right time. Mostly, we'd just bob about, drift through London like ghosts, talk about our band and admire the city's shape; it seemed magical to us. Sitting outside pubs in Soho on long summer evenings, climbing the park fence at eleven at night in winter, that stillness among the firs, grass crunching beneath your feet.

Other times Peter and I would just work away, on the peripheries of the scene, made all the more aware of that fact by the near misses we had. One night, I remember being elbowed in the ribs by Liam Gallagher. I was in the Dublin Castle innocently minesweeping drinks into my pint glass at the time. I looked around. He was accompanied by Mani from The Stone Roses and Finley Quaye; you could almost hear the sound of a hundred necks craning to get a better look at them all. Peter approached Liam and said something to him which I couldn't make out, though Liam's voice cut across the room: 'I'm the Devil's dick, me.' But Liam didn't mean anything by the accidental elbow, graciously bought me a beer and then politely declined to come back to our flat and have a jam. I can fully understand that, now that I've so frequently been on the receiving end of such requests. It was impossible for me to understand, then, that he was just a person in the pub enjoying a drink with his friends. Not the rock star, not the performer, just the Devil's dick enjoying a pint.

Another night, we liberated a moped on the Kentish Town Road, a Honda Cub 90 propped up outside the WKD Café, a dive full of indie kids being scrunched by bouncers. WKD stood for Wisdom, Knowledge and Destiny, which were hardly abounding in there. It didn't last long. The moped had been sitting outside for a while, obviously abandoned or dumped, and the third time we walked past we decided to wheel it with us. Down a backstreet, Peter was walking along and I was sitting on it, sort of wheeling it along, and then we got leapt upon. I remember this Kiwi man, a sort of angry, apish figure waving a police badge at us, the headlights of a car screaming up the road. It was like something from *The Sweeney*. Scary stuff, it jolted us out of our reverie and then some. We were arrested and carted off down to the cells. When they asked us what we did, I said I was an actor and Peter said he was a poet. I think it was then that they realized that we weren't professional criminals. The police officer at the desk was from Liverpool so I instantly tried on my bad Scouse accent, trying to impress upon her how Peter and I weren't vagrants – that we shared a house, that there were lots of books in our toilet. A little too Withnailian now that I think about it, but I couldn't stop myself. I asked her if she read on the toilet, or did they call it the can in Liverpool? At the end of it I think we kind of charmed them, but they still banged us up in the cells anyway.

Once we'd stopped protesting our innocence, I think we were charged with the theft of an automobile. I still have the charge sheets somewhere. I think we were both shocked when they actually shut the cell doors on us. They had small chalkboards outside the cells, and on the way through we liberated the chalk next to the boards through the little shutter in the door and Peter wrote poetry on the walls. We left our mark as we thought Libertines should. We were released the next day with a caution; by all accounts the bike's owner was less than pleased that we'd liberated his Honda.

But we were Libertines: we liberated. That was what we did. We always did know how to make our own fun.

TWO

Plan A

It's late at night, and I'm sitting at the kitchen table. Another cigarette, another glass of red wine ... there's tea on the table, too, but that's cooling. When I set out to write this book and this solo album I really didn't know what I was getting myself into. I unearthed some journals that I'd long ago put away, out of sight and mind, and was flicking through the pages, and they fell open to reveal four photo-booth pictures still in a strip. Two of Peter and two of me: we'd shared the booth, running in and out so we could get two shots apiece. We look impossibly young; I'm cocky about something, or pretending to be, and Peter's a shock of hair and eyes like a deer. A few pages later and there's some truly terrible poetry, a sketch of Peter that he hated (but sketched when I was hating him so that's fair enough) and then some words I recognize as being the genesis of 'Death On The Stairs'.

I've just been watching the young me play *Top of the Pops* for the first time. I usually can't face watching myself sober, so I'll get drunk and go online to look at past glories, and am occasionally pleasantly surprised to find that some have hardly faded at all. I can't believe it now, but when we were offered a spot performing on that British institution, we began arguing about the rights and wrongs of doing it. We really wanted to – for egotistical reasons we were dying to be on national TV, and you don't join a band like The Libertines to be a shrinking violet – but then someone said that The Clash had refused to do it. God knows what relevance that had, but it seemed really important to us at the time, and someone else said that Pan's People, or whoever it was, had danced to 'Bankrobber' in their absence, and that that was even worse . . . As if that had any fucking bearing on us at all: I think this was the first moment I realized how intrinsically self-important bands are. Everything has to be analysed, ruminated upon, done to fucking death. It's all so massive and important, so Spinal Tap at times. Forget the devil being in the detail: all the bands I've been in are stuck in the fucking cracks.

Anyone could tell we wanted to do *Top of the Pops*. Who wouldn't? We only had to talk ourselves into it. Our egos won that battle, along with me saying that if there's one kid in Wigan who's going to tap into what we're doing because of it, while he's eating his beans in front of the telly, then we've achieved something. We did 'Time For Heroes' that first appearance. It was back in the exact same BBC building where I'd stalked the corridors in my trilby trying to impress posh girls, so that was a little victory in its way. We did *Top of the Pops* again, a second appearance on the show, but that doesn't get talked about so much because Peter wasn't there. Peter hated Anthony for a while – Anthony Rossomando who replaced him for some of the live shows – because Anthony did *Top of the Pops* in his place. Peter accidentally saw it on telly, and he was at his lowest ebb at the time, and it understandably tore him up a bit.

Even back then I avoided watching myself doing 'Time For Heroes' on the TV until I was good and drunk. When I did, I watched it out of one eye while listing slightly and it was all right; it looked like we were winning. Quite soon after, I met Graham Coxon from Blur for the first time, which was a big deal for me. He'd seen it, too, and he said he loved my 'anti-guitar solo', which I didn't really understand but decided to take as an enormous compliment anyway. I tried to maintain my composure, but I can't explain the feeling of happiness it gave me. When Coxon was a drinker and he was in the Good Mixer pretty much holding up the bar, our bass player, John, had gone up to him and asked him if he was Graham Coxon. Graham said to him that if he didn't know the answer to that then he could fuck off, which makes a lot of sense in a way. Though that didn't help John much; he was gutted.

There was a similar frisson of excitement when we got played in the Queen Vic for the first time, too. Like *Top of the Pops*, *EastEnders* crosses those boundaries, it helps explain to your parents and family what it is you actually do because, in the real world, playing and singing in a band is not working for a living. So when your family's sitting watching Pat behind the bar, or whoever it was running the Vic at that point, and the jukebox starts playing 'Can't Stand Me Now', it helps people close to you to understand. Before then, they'd say, 'Have you met anyone famous, have you met Britney?' But getting a record deal doesn't give you the keys to some secret half of London, to the parties where Bono hangs out with Britney. And thank fuck for that. The Vic's a good way to help a different generation understand another world, and maybe a good benchmark for your family, so they can start taking you seriously, and maybe get off your back a little bit. It was like giving my dad a gold disc: an affirmation I think we'd both been looking for. So I raised a glass when we snaked out of the speakers in the Queen Vic. These days, it doesn't seem like such a big deal, though I always regretted never catching sight of us on one of those band posters they have pasted up by Walford East Tube station. And this from the man who debated if being on *Top of the Pops* was selling out.

* * *

My parents broke up when I was five years old. I didn't see it coming, but I suppose I heard it. Our house was filled with shouting, things were broken, stuff was hurled across rooms. I'm sure nobody got badly hurt, though I'm certain some feelings were. I'd come into the living room to studied silence and a smashed mug in the corner of the room, shards like chipped teeth across the carpet. My mother would be staring hard out of the window, my father in the kitchen busying himself with something, the kettle announcing morning with its shrill whistle. The noise abated quickly when my mother left for good, and there was a hole in our household then that filled up with sadness. My father seemed shrunken somehow, but that must be in my imagination. I'm not sure a five-year-old could have truly understood what was going on. All I knew was that I missed my mother, and I'd stare out at the estate we lived on and imagine her making her way back towards us through the hedgerows and houses, and how she'd catch me staring and wave. Then my dad would tell me to get dressed and pull me from my reverie.

When I was born, we were living on an estate in Basingstoke, and the birth was a particularly protracted and painful one by all accounts. There were two of us; I was the unexpected twin, or the uninvited guest as I sometimes think of it. My brother died a few months later and I don't want to labour over this, but I don't want to deny it either; it's something that's stuck with me all my life. What if he'd lived, and what if he were here with me now? Did my living have something to do with his dying? I've always stayed close to one person since – I'm not sure if that's coincidence, or even relevant – but there's been Peter, and there's been Chris and Anthony and Kieran Leonard (the lithest man I have ever met, a screaming and tender troubadour – a scruffy Cobainesque comrade in striped skintight *Beetlejuice* trousers, big boots and a razor-sharp wit). Not to put too fine a point on it, I've always needed someone near. My big sister's two years older than me – so I was born with a boss – and we grew close as cups were thrown and doors slammed shut, and our parents banged up and down the stairs.

My mother might as well have disappeared into the ether for a year or so after she left; she adopted what I'd come to think of as a happy hippy lifestyle, a transient freewheeling. We lost her to a commune, a number of communes over the years as a matter of fact, and so, for the next eight years or thereabouts, I lived between two places. School days with my dad at our house in Whitchurch, and most weekends and holidays out at a commune or in a field under the stars. It certainly wasn't without its charms, but there was such a stark and unexpected contrast between my two lives; I'd literally feel the jolt as I made the transition between the two worlds.

I've come to regard those times very fondly. I was blessed to be torn between two such different ways of life, to be exposed to all of these colours; my formative palette was surely enriched by it. What I most remember about the communes at first is looking up and seeing all this hair, men with huge beards and wild, untamed hair everywhere. I go back and look at photos from that time now and it looks like fun, quite a groovy scene, but at the time I found it peculiar. I'd make them laugh by complaining about it all, about the smell and having to sit around in the dark with people farting. It didn't feel particularly liberating, but then I suppose they were on their own journey. They used to respond to my moaning by laughing and saying, 'Isn't it priceless the stuff that kids come out with?' But I reckon kids quite often come out with the truth, as they haven't yet learnt to censor themselves. Farting and sitting around in the dark aside, there was a lot of hand-holding and embracing; spiritual meditation, New Age philosophies, that sort of thing. And lots and lots of music. I remember the sound of people meditating, the 'Om' reverberating through the tents as the nights drew in. There were lots of drugs, though I only ever really saw the effect they had on people – blissed-out faces all around and glazed eyes staring off into the depths of the universe. It was – and this is an understatement on a grand scale – a very colourful landscape for a young child. Very conducive to the development of an imaginative and inquiring mind. I don't think it did me any harm; more opened me up to things. And then the inevitable jolt, the return to my home on the council estate with its well-defined rules, structured days and, most importantly, stability.

I am nostalgic about my childhood days, yes, but it's not entirely unalloyed fondness I bounced between, feeling pretty bereft emotionally. I know both my parents tried very hard in difficult circumstances, but I was very aware that I was missing some sort of a loving linchpin in my life. I wanted someone I could turn to, someone to lean on and trust. My dad was working all the time on various artistic things and working hard to help the family get by, although he carried a simmering anger around with him, which I may or may not have inherited. Meanwhile, my mum was off being a totally different person, a different kind of parent. I think my sister and I felt cast adrift a little, as if we didn't belong to either. I needed the stability of my dad's world, but I was never hugged or cuddled there as a child, while, in the other world, the world of free love and enlightenment, everyone hugged you to the point that it became meaningless. In The Libertines people never stopped hugging me. I'm pretty good at hugging, actually; the five-year-old in me throws himself at it as if it's salvation.

* * *

Looking back through the fog, I'm grateful for *Top of the Pops* and the Queen Vic. Our deal with Rough Trade brought us that kind of presence, and saved me and Peter from bedsits without doors and other people's basements. It was more than we could have hoped for at the beginning, especially when, at a certain point in our development, the early line-up of The Libertines fell apart.

We'd been drifting like tumbleweed across London, taking our own sweet time, playing beautiful, flowery songs and singing about love's vicissitudes, lugging amps into old people's homes, and doing little gigs wherever we could. It all broke up, though, when Peter began to change gigs around, cancel shows and refuse to take money for performing. The original drummer and bassist were too ambitious to take this, so they quit and the bottom fell out, but we stuck with our manager and, when we saw what The Strokes were doing, we began to form a different idea of the band. I think when The Strokes broke so suddenly and so big, we were rather fancifully annoyed at them: annoyed they were shagging our women and taking our drugs, taking the space that, in our minds, was reserved for us. We decided something had to be done, and so we began to write new songs. They were faster and more driven – sexier, more tortured, funnier – and everything began to click. I remember the time well because there was a Rough Trade showcase looming on the horizon, which we were due to play in, and I was at a friend's flat teaching Johnny Borrell the bass line to 'Horrorshow'. It was the day the planes hit the World Trade Center Twin Towers in New York, and only a few weeks before the showcase. Johnny was originally our bassist but, when the day of that showcase came, I phoned him as I was arriving at Earl's Court, to see if he was almost there. Johnny, though, was on the Alabama 3 tour bus in Cardiff, in the middle of a rather large bender, so we had to do the showcase with me playing the fucking bass. Thankfully, it still worked, and Rough Trade took us on. Gary, a session drummer who'd played most famously with Eddie Grant, was working in marketing at that point – he was our manager's secretary's boyfriend – and he came on board, too. Rough Trade then pointed out that we needed a bassist, so we asked John. And that was The Libertines fully formed in its second, famous, incarnation. We'd found a rich seam of new songs, which we continued to mine for the first single and album, but when we got to the second album the old ones started to sneak back in. 'Music When The Lights Go Out' is a song that has its roots in the quieter, poetic first incarnation of the band. It was great, after the angry thing, to have such a reservoir of wonderful rich, lyrical material that we'd really wanted to sing about when we were young, fresh and idealistic.

Signing for Rough Trade was amazing, as well as a real relief after all those years of slumming it with our intricate little melodies and beautiful words. We'd come back with an attitude and anger, as if on the rebound after the years during which people hadn't wanted us: a very genuine sense of frustration followed, suddenly, by that incredible connection, and we weren't going to let it pass. Thanks to Rough Trade, Peter and I moved east to Bethnal Green, to the next Albion Rooms, and it was domestic bliss after a fashion. We shared a business bank account and the flat, a beautiful place that had one big room upstairs and one tiny little cupboard. Nevertheless, it was spacious and bright, and the main room – Peter's room – housed the most amazing brass bed. I know that because I saw it every time I went through it to get to my bedroom (the cupboard). All I ever wanted in that flat was a proper door to my room. Peter's room was always filled with noise: records or guitars or repeats of

Steptoe and Son and *Rising Damp* on TV. We had a modest fridge, which never housed anything other than booze and £50 notes. We'd never handled large amounts of £50 notes before so we luxuriated in them, ironing them and placing them in the fridge. It was very cinematic opening up a fridge and seeing all that money in neat, colourful piles. It sounds vulgar in hindsight, but it was actually quite innocent. When the Dollar Man, our dealer, came around we'd pluck a couple of fifties out of the fridge, press them on our faces for that cooling sensation and hand them over. We liked him: he had a gold tooth and wore shades, just like you'd want a drug dealer to. It was while we were in Bethnal Green that I came home one day and saw our record contract sitting on the table. And I thought that Peter must have been getting nostalgic, revelling in the moment when we got picked up, looking at the paperwork that sealed our deal, and thinking how far we'd come. And then I saw my chequebook, open, with a cheque missing; and next to that a piece of paper with lots of different versions of my signature directly lifted off the contract. Peter hadn't even tried to hide the fact that he'd forged my signature; I quite admired him for that. I admired his spirit.

* * *

Even when Peter wasn't forging my signature, I'm about as adept with money as the World Bank – by which I mean not at all. I started off being frugal and I've always been a hard worker. I went out to work as soon as I was allowed, and had a whole range of awful, dangerous or soul-destroying jobs, factory jobs cleaning sump oil, or tossing salad in a huge warehouse under barbaric lights. Nevertheless, they got me out of the house, and they were happy hours. It was great to be alone and isolated even in the company of others and the idea of actually being paid opened up a new world for me. Earning your first wage is an amazing feeling, even if I wasn't great at the jobs I unearthed.

There were rumours in that salad-packing factory that there were black widow spiders in the crates, and part of our job was to pick fat moths out from between the green salad leaves, put them in a polythene bag provided expressly for that purpose and not give them a second thought as they expired. Someone found half a frog once, and they had to stop the whole load, shut everything down, and there was another enduring rumour that a frozen body had once fallen out of one of the crates of imported leaves. Some poor bugger had been trying to get into the country illegally and had chosen the wrong method of entry. I imagined him shattering on impact with the floor, like someone caught in liquid nitrogen in a movie, shattering into a thousand pieces, shining limbs skittering away across the factory. The reality, if it had ever happened, had probably been an urgent call to HR and a screaming workmate being led quietly out of the door.

The factory was about three miles outside Whitchurch, and I worked the graveyard shift, which meant cycling through country lanes with no streetlights, and I'd hope for nights with a full moon as that made my journey easier. I'd zone out and use my peripheral vision to sense where the road was, my gears snagging as I puffed my way to work. I'd arrive around ten in the evening, the salad factory floodlit and looming before me like a UFO that had dropped out of the sky, white clouds drifting upwards, glowing eerily in the halogen lights. I'd climb into my white overalls and wellies, feeling like the sperm in the Woody Allen film *Everything You Always Wanted To Know About Sex But Were Afraid To Ask*, pull the hairnet tight over my head and apply some alcohol rub. The latter was easily the most fascinating aspect of the job: get too close, inhale too deeply and the strip lighting overhead grew briefly, if brilliantly, bright and my heartbeat would fill my head. Then I'd trudge towards the gigantic fridge, where the conveyer belts ran on an endless loop and huge bins of salad sailed by like a low-rent *Generation Game*. The strip lighting that bloomed with alcohol rub made everyone look gnarled and zombie-like and cruel. Features washed out, eyes glinting like cheap glass; smiles became grimaces, a cheery wink an indication of impending evil. Admittedly, I was seventeen and sleepless, but it wasn't just my imagination that was making ghouls of the workforce. I did that for a year and the thing that stays with me the most isn't the sheer inanity of the tasks I was asked to do or even the chemical rub: it was the piped music that came in through the refrigerated walls. Alanis Morissette's 'Jagged Little Pill'. It had just been released and what was worse than hearing it over and over again was only just being able to make it out and then it got lost in the drone of heavy machinery. In reality none of us had a clue what we were doing, but the salad would slow in front of us on the conveyor and we'd toss it and then send it on its way to who knows where. I'd imagine people unpacking their lunch and biting into their sandwiches across the country, never giving a thought to the aimless shuffling of salad leaves by drones like me on quiet nights in the Hampshire countryside. You couldn't really talk to anyone unless you were willing to shout so I'd get lost in myself, just thinking of elaborate ways to entertain myself. At first, I pretended to the woman who did the coat checks that I had a mental disorder and I always had to wear two of everything. So I started off by wearing a watch on each wrist and slowly added bits and pieces until, by the end of it, I was wearing two pairs of trousers and two coats. On reflection, I might have taken it too far, but that's where I went when I got lost in my thoughts. All there was to do was think, reflect on where you were, how you had got there and how you could get out. I'd just think and think, until it was five in the morning and the day was reaching in and I made my weary way home, the bike's spinning wheels beneath me.

When I finally got out it was on my own terms, even if I was wearing three layers of clothes. Unlike in my first job from which I'd been fired, aged thirteen, for my own good. At £2 an hour I'd been cleaning the bins and machinery in a plastic mouldings factory. The sun used to come in through the ventilation grills in the ceiling, as did the rain that collected in gleaming, oily puddles on the floor. Years later I'd see the *Alien* movie and recognize the interior of the *Nostromo*, there among the greasy steel moulds and unmoving machines that bent plastic to their will. I'd run a rag carelessly along them, the only movement among the stillness, a strange, and in retrospect, dangerous and illegal idyll.

* * *

Once I'd escaped the sleepy, dulling routines of Whitchurch, and Peter and I were living together, just starting to feel our way with the band, my grip on money loosened. I remember the day the Giro came we'd go mad. Suddenly we'd be dining like kings on oysters and champagne for twenty-four hours, and I recall once taking tea at an upmarket tea room, all porcelain and sponge cake and cucumber sandwiches without crusts. Peter had looked at his watch and said, 'We're late, come on. We must go.' And, at that, he stabbed his cigarette out in his tea, took a final sip, and then upped and left, no doubt whisking me along to our next money-burning appointment. To me, that was just devastatingly cool. Then, when all the benefit money was gone, we'd slum it for a fortnight. It'd be back to minesweeping drinks in Camden. I don't know how we didn't go completely mad when we first made any real money. I think, on my part, it simply came down to base avarice. Peter used to joke about how much I loved my DVD collection. So, when I first had some spare cash, I bought a computer that played DVDs, and a new suit, and then dived straight into another shop for a *Fawlty Towers* box set and some David Niven films, too.

The importance of those old British films to me shouldn't be underestimated. I've only ever written songs about escape – I don't write about the here and now, I want to be transported, and to take people with me to some fantastical place – and that's what cinema has always represented to me. Peter Sellers, the inimitable David Niven, Sir Alec Guinness, Charles Laughton, they all knew how to take me away. To a generation, Alec Guinness is the righteous knight at the heart of *Star Wars*, but to me he's the ultimate comic actor and chameleon: the D'Ascoyne family in *Kind Hearts and Coronets*, the shadowy villain in *The Ladykillers*. There's something about him, something so quintessentially English. It's strange to think that a leading man these days is rarely out of his twenties and they were all pushing on into their late forties. Some would say change is for the better, but I'm not sure I'd agree.

All of those actors were role models but David Niven stands out because, when I watched his films, I couldn't help but see my grandfather on the screen. They looked the same to me, sounded the same, carried themselves in the same way, so much so that, when I was little I truly thought Niven and my granddad might be the same man. I found Niven's autobiography, *The Moon's a Balloon*, in a charity shop when I was living in the Albion Rooms, sharing a basement with Peter, and it became a treasured possession, taking pride of place in our one big room with a mattress on the floor, and I'd sit there, reading it by candlelight. The whole book is charming: even when he's talking about blundering into his first sexual experiences, the death of his father, his friendship with a prostitute, he has a certain grace. He was a noble and dignified gent, a symbol for me of a lost art, a lost way of being, a lost Englishness. Like Niven, the Marx Brothers have the power to make me feel momentarily elated. They found the goodness in things, too. When my glass is half empty, when I'm trying my damnedest to see the light and failing, I can watch Niven come up that beach in *A Matter of Life and Death* or watch the Marx Brothers horse around in *Animal Crackers* and feel their rare magic jolt me back to life. Peter liked the Marx Brothers, too, and we'd watch their films on the bus, to help us forget the relentless miles slipping by under our prone bodies.

DVDs, then, were my first vice with Peter, the first thing I splurged money on, and it seems strange to me now that it took me a while to splash out on a nice guitar. I remember the day I did, however. Peter and I went down to Vintage & Rare, the pair of us as pleased as punch and practically glowing with pride, both very naïve. The proprietor must have seen us coming, because he was standing behind the counter rubbing his hands together with glee. I bought my Melody Maker, which I still use, and Peter bought the Epiphone Coronet, which I believe his father impounded for reasons that still escape me.

Even though he'd ultimately kick my door in and try to steal my stuff, Peter gave me security and confidence to go out and do that, to believe that I could go out on a limb, even in prosaic, financial matters. When we were really firing on all cylinders and were together then it really felt like no one could touch us, and that nothing else mattered. As much as I try to deflect it, play it down and be English about it, there was a very powerful romance and beauty to our friendship. At the beginning it was pure and uncomplicated; there was a chemistry. Together we were a complete unit, in each other's company quite different from how we were with other people. I can sit here as the shadows get longer and be diffident about it until the sun comes up again tomorrow morning, but the fact is that if that dynamic between us hadn't existed none of this would have happened, I wouldn't be lamenting what I lost – what we both lost – I wouldn't be writing it all down. When we're together and we can forget about bullshit, we become two old souls, kindred spirits in seclusion.

* * *

Enough of lamenting what we'd lost, though. When we signed to Rough Trade, it was all just beginning, and before we'd had a chance to realize what was happening, The Libertines were on the cover of the *NME*. The new deal with Rough Trade had brought us a new family, not least in the shape of our press officer, Tony the Tiger, a lovely man whose mum knew him better as Tony Lincoln, a man who always wore a backpack, even with a suit. I found that charming. He made an effort to take us aside just before our *NME* cover photo was due, when the single was getting played on radio stations, and he said, in the nicest possible way, 'You do you know, after this Wednesday, that things are going to be very different, don't you? As soon as this cover comes out you're going to be very, very famous. I've seen this before, so just prepare yourselves.'

How did we prepare ourselves? You can get the *NME* in the West End on a Tuesday, a day before it gets sent around the country, so, come Tuesday, Peter and I reconvene at home in Bethnal Green, suited, booted, sunglasses, acting absurdly cool, and take the Tube to Tottenham Court Road station. Sure enough, there we are, on the front cover, on display on a little news-stand opposite the Astoria. So we ask for a couple of copies, give a knowing nod to the woman behind the counter and then ... nothing. Peter very slowly takes the change from her hand and tries to meet her eye, and she just smiles at us and moves on to the next customer. We spent all day walking around clutching copies of the *NME*, cover out, and nothing happened that day, or that week, not a sausage. It was a fallacy, a funny one, but a fallacy nevertheless.

I'm not quite sure what we were expecting, but, when we broke, we broke big and we broke quickly. We stepped up to the plate and swung, as an American fellow told me as we stepped off stage at the Astoria, the very place, only months before, we'd been to buy the *NME*. We were supporting The Vines; it was meant to be their first headline show at the venue, but they pulled out and we got top billing by default. That's when I realized that we were breaking – no one, but *no one*, gave their tickets back, and as we stepped out it was if they were there to see us. Even the balcony was a mass of adoring silhouettes. We stepped up to the plate and swung. These are the inescapable moments.

All of a sudden, we were recording our first single for Rough Trade with Bernard Butler. Initially, Peter was in thrall to Bernard: he placed him on a pedestal in many ways. As a young man Peter was an *NME* boy, a letter writer, and Bernard was the cover star, someone who, as part of Suede, helped change the musical landscape for a while. I remember Rough Trade brought him along and he was wearing his

50

Converse and had a big parka on; he was looking very Bernard Butler, which endeared him to me. I sometimes want people to look and act like my perception of them, like the picture I hold of them in my head. When I meet people, fans who stop me for a photo in the street or people who just want to say hello, I always hope that I come away and leave with them the impression they'd hoped for. So, in one way, Bernard was the man we hoped he'd be, quite a player, amazing style. He was also very, very methodical and slightly schoolmasterly in his production approach, which I also found charming. He was like some cool, floppy-haired teacher whose lesson you always secretly looked forward to. And we needed it at first, that hands-on approach, making sure all the boxes were ticked.

Later on, we also worked with Bernard to record 'Don't Look Back Into The Sun' and he and Peter got on less well. I think Peter was getting tired of the prescriptive approach: it was only when Peter felt that he'd outgrown that way of doing things that it all turned a bit nasty. Strangely enough, that was exactly the same time as all the crack and the brown business started happening. The constant niggling of my nerves ensured that I never fully enjoyed the studio, as I was always so nervous as to what the results of our labours might be. Somehow, in that second session, we managed to pull it all together, and get everything done with Bernard that we were meant to, thanks mainly to Bernard playing guitar parts and doing backing on the songs that Peter hadn't showed up to finish. We were having to edit together one or two particularly bad vocal takes, stitching things together and doctoring it afterwards, putting in more work than we really should have had to. But what could we do? During those sessions, Peter wasn't playing ball at all really. At one point he stopped coming to the studio altogether. We'd show up at two in the afternoon and stay until about two in the morning and our eyes would occasionally drift towards the door, but he rarely walked through it during that fortnight we spent there.

Mick Jones, who produced *Up The Bracket*, and also our second album, *The Libertines*, was instantly one of the boys when he worked with us, much more a part of the gang. Everyone took to him. He was a musical hero to the other guys, but I genuinely didn't know that much about the music he'd made. I mean, I'm the guy who told him to think about changing the mix on 'Guns Of Brixton' because I thought it was his new stuff and needed tweaking. I suggested he get rid of the 'poing' noise. To his credit he let it go, but I thought the rest of the band might jump me. At the end of each day's session, he'd give us a crash course in The Clash. We'd all put our feet up after recording, someone would nip out to the supermarket and grab some beers and they'd talk me through the catalogue, a few punk pointers here and there. I really enjoyed it. My enduring memory of a lot of those sessions is looking through the glass and Mick taking it all very seriously sitting there with his pen and pad and a huge joint on the go – either that, or doing his famous dance. Both are reassuring images to me.

* * *

But I'm getting ahead of myself. That first single, the double A side of 'What A Waster' and 'I Get Along', came out in June 2002, and in August we played the Reading Festival for the first time. We were the opening band on the Evening Session Stage, and it felt like a dream, a bad dream, the ones where you're naked in front of a crowd and there's nothing you can do about it. It was the wrong place at the wrong time, around midday and swelteringly hot, and even from the wings you could see that the tent was packed. We were in our ascendancy and the drunk blokes and the girls on their shoulders chanting our name only served to confirm that. It was the first time that my family had come en masse to see me, too, so I was jumpy, doubly on edge with the pressure of the show and my mum and dad being among the expectant faces out front. So we started, and, as in most cases when we were a bit on edge, we just threw ourselves into it, and suddenly it all felt like it was clicking into place and I began to enjoy the fact that it was summer time and here we were on the Reading stage and it was packed out for us. And then without warning our backline went down. I'm not sure if my amp blew up or not, but it gave up the ghost with something that sounded like a sigh. We were two songs in, I'd just started windmilling the arms, giving it some oomph, and then nothing. So we just had to stop and wait while this tech called Barry changed the amp for the spare that didn't really work. And I literally didn't know what to do. It was one of my biggest nightmares, standing there silently in front of the crowd. They were looking at us and I was looking right back at them, pacing around like an expectant father. We didn't really have the confidence, and hadn't learnt that level of professional showmanship to start a singalong, or make a joke. That was something we'd all learn later on. The seconds ticked by like hours. A terrible cliché, but true, when there are thousands of disgruntled punters staring at you, and you know your dad's out in the middle of them, quite probably tut-tutting to himself. In reality, we only stopped for about five minutes, but that's still a chunk of a forty-minute set and, to make up for it, we came back on with added vigour, which led to extra buffeting between me and Peter. We were really running at each other, crashing into each other mid-stage, giving the mic stand hell. Anything was allowed, really, but the main thing was to avoid the heads of the guitar. We were thundering through 'I Get Along', buoyed up by our collective energy, giving it everything we had, colliding like particles, launching ourselves into orbit and banging into each other in the middle. Peter would come charging in, and I'd sort of brace myself, but not too much, because you didn't want it to be too staged, you wanted to keep the genuine beauty and flow going and John, sensibly, stayed out of the way while all this was going on. Stoic and still and very handsome, that's what you need in a bass player, I think. Towards the song's climax, we ran into each other at the side of the stage, bounced together against what had previously appeared to be a wall, and then disappeared through it out of sight as the canvas gave way. And that was it, goodnight and good luck. Peter managed to haul himself back onto the lip of the stage, which made my father angry – I think he suspected some kind of bullying in the band, but in reality it was just part of our thing. I'm surprised we didn't fall off stage more, now that I think about it. But the fall felt like redemption. We'd managed to pull it back from the brink, to get past the potential humiliation, nerves and the confusion and to overcome, to conquer the audience in our own special way.

Now the events of that day seem fatefully funny, almost like a Marx Brothers' sketch, though I won't deny that falling off the side of the stage was a little bit embarrassing, especially as I was sort of semi-throttled by a guitar lead around my neck as I rolled over the edge, like a condemned man swinging down through the trapdoor. The audience didn't get to see that bit, thankfully; they just saw this rather extraordinary stage exit. We'd fired them up and they were riotous by all accounts.

The next gig didn't go so well. We'd travelled up to Leeds to play the second leg of the festival. Peter kicked me up the arse on stage and we ended up coming to blows over it. His comedy kick wasn't a new thing, and it always wound me up. It wasn't the physical pain – there wasn't really any – it was more the humiliation. When you're giving your heart to a melody and you believe you're really connecting with something spiritual, tuning into something higher . . . then you hear the crowd laugh and you turn around to see Peter doing a Charlie Chaplin kick up your bum, it's a little bit insulting.

Now, I firmly believe there is a time and a place for Charlie Chaplin, but it's not on the stage at Leeds in the middle of a Libertines set. Charlie Chaplin has always been one of my heroes. I had a copy of *Modern Times* on video when I was nineteen, but I really fell in love with him a few years later. I was on tour and Rotterdam had offered up its usual vices and found me wanting. I stood next to the local promoter and he held my gaze as he detailed precisely how, between them, the Luftwaffe and the RAF had levelled the city during the Second World War. I imagined the bombs falling, the plumes of steaming water rising up in the bay, wood cracking in the heat, shots being exchanged. Later, I was rolling drunkenly around the town with this at the back of my mind when I spotted an innocuous looking door in an alleyway. I wish I could tell you that it led me to Narnia, but, to me, it was better than meeting a talking lion. The blackboard above the door simply said 'Chaplin' and, as I pushed my way into the darkness, the room fell back to reveal a cinema screen, a full orchestra and *Modern Times* about to start. I sat there in the blackness as Rotterdam disappeared from my thoughts and Chaplin wove his unique magic, the rising swell of the orchestra's strings and brass carrying me away. I was instantly and absolutely hooked, floating happily in another universe, another time. Charlie Chaplin was the first Englishman to conquer the world and he did it with love. I heard a story that in Cuba in the 1960s they erected a screen in a backwater town square and showed *Modern Times* to people who had never seen a moving image before. They had no idea who he was and everyone, different generations together, was dumbfounded by it, by him. I once made a girlfriend watch *The Great Dictator* and she resisted at first, but was soon drawn in, inching towards the edge of the sofa as if she were going to reach out and touch the screen. It's simple beauty reaching out across the years and the final speech echoing down the ages. Even Hitler got Chaplin; even he was entranced by Chaplin's innate goodness – and, by coincidence, they were born only days apart. It means a lot to me that one generation of my family lived in Lambeth the same time as Chaplin did, though I'm sure they never passed in the street or saw each other in the shops. It's enough for me to know they shared the same space. They're funny things, heroes. I have very few. I guess the only one still alive is Lou Reed, now that Beryl Reid and Oliver Reed have shuffled off their mortal coils . . .

*　*　*

But I digress. I think that day in Leeds, after Reading's triumphant exit stage left, I was coming down from a mountain of coke and what amounted to a great victory for us, one of the first. Peter was elated about what a fine show we'd done, but I felt angry, aggrieved and down. Maybe Peter hadn't meant any harm, and it is likely I was volatile and oversensitive that afternoon and that I was letting the hangover and the comedown get the better of me. I didn't let go of my anger about the kick, probably hammed it up a bit for the onlookers' benefit, in fact, and he began to get upset that I wasn't enjoying it all like I should have been until, without thinking, we lunged for each other, and Gary grabbed my hair and pulled my head backwards. Peter piled in with fists flailing: I got quite the clout thanks to Gary's kind intervention. So, rather childishly, I ran away and cried a little, but it was the kind of crying you do when you're waiting for someone to find you and ask what you're crying about. It was just like being a kid all over again. We then had to get the same bus back to London and, after a little while, we were all friends again, but it was my fault for tainting that really. I did and I do take the blame for that.

* * *

It's funny that, even though the band was becoming all-consuming and starting to get out of control, we could still carry on in our same old ways. One moment that particularly stands out is an ill-considered trip to France, a fool's errand into the night. The Formule 1 chain of hotels is, I think I can say without fear of a lawyer landing on me, less than salubrious. If you've yet to experience the delights of this ever-expanding chain, the rooms are moulded out of one big plastic frame, the sink and the beds an integral part of the actual wall. I imagine that, once you've taken the bedding out, you can clean the whole thing in one go with a high-powered hose, like a festival toilet. Innovative, yes, but it felt to me as if we'd been banged up again. The bunk beds came with plastic mattresses that scratched at your skin with every turn. I looked across at Peter and his friend La. I wasn't sure what we were doing there, and even less certain about La's part in things. La liked brown, too; he was one of Peter's shadier companions, and his being there made me feel even itchier than the mattress did. A white hotel room made of plastic, and two heroin smokers in a restricted space: who doesn't love a road trip?

We were on our way to record a session in Nantes for two French guys we'd met in a bar in London. Our first album was out and making some waves, so I suppose we can blame the booze we'd been drinking for agreeing to work with two Frenchman we'd never set eyes on before. They were quite provocative as I recall, telling us that we thought we were really big news but that we should go to France and record something real with them, for a small label they owned. Peter and I kept saying yes to everything – it's like we wanted to star in our own unbelievable sitcom or farce – so we ended up in a freezing barn on the outskirts of Nantes that was supposedly doubling as a studio. La, it transpired, was meant to be producing the sessions – the same La who'd never produced a record in his life; but there was always a job for someone who's carrying brown around.

We did four songs out there. I remember really not wanting to go, as I didn't have a passport at the time and I was happy in London with my then girlfriend, quietly enjoying the first real fruits of our labour with our debut album. But Peter really laid it on, saying that if I didn't go along then he'd leave the band and that would be it. I was forced to cross the Channel using my sister's passport, so I had to sit in the back of the car with my hair in my face pretending to be asleep as we got on the ferry, just so that we could go to a derelict barn to record songs for two men we didn't even know. We arrived on the Continent and snow was falling thickly. It was blowing a miserable gale and it didn't even feel like an adventure. It just felt dumb. A few years down the line, the song 'Narcissist' from those sessions surfaced on our second album, but that could quite have easily been recorded at home in London, in a room where the windows worked and the snow didn't get in. The other songs have since been posted online, but they were never really released. We never made things easy for ourselves. I've been told since that's part of our charm.

* * *

In the grand scheme of things, a band's a speck. It's nothing. But it's also chaos, excitement and expectation. We were on an upward trajectory, but you can't properly feel it at the time. In a way, I wish we had experienced that thrill, the thrill of the booster rockets falling away, knowing that this was the upside and the downside was coming. You're getting more popular, more and more people are coming to the shows, but you've no idea when you might level out, what that feels like, when you reach the apex of your flight and the only way to go is back down. I feel pressure oppressively and, even then, I was beginning to feel a bit like Atlas with the world on his shoulders, trying to keep my dreams alive.

THREE

There and Back Again

Before The Libertines, I hadn't really travelled. I didn't board an aeroplane until I was twenty-two and didn't taste hummus until twenty-five. I'll qualify that: I didn't even know what hummus was until I was twenty-five. We didn't have the money to travel, and the communes and camps with my mother felt like small holidays in themselves – though that was the thinking of a kid who'd never even been on a package trip. My grandparents took it on themselves to take my sister and me away when they could. I remember one listless summer when I was seven years old at the Lakeside Holiday Camp on Hayling Island on the Hampshire coast. I was floating in a canoe, my grandparents close by on the shore, the plastic paddle flashing against the sun shining on the water and my hand just breaking the surface when it brushed up against a jellyfish and got stung. I remember the swelling and the tears and my sister's gentle words shushing and comforting me. In the ballroom at night I'd squirm as the adults passed balloons between their knees or sat on the floor and pretended to row a boat. They'd try to get me to do the hokey cokey and I'd run and hide behind my grandparents and cry, horrified to be trapped in a *Hi-de-Hi!* universe.

Later, my stepmum and Dad took us up to a lonely house they'd rented in Scotland, which I remember for the moors, the different shades of green and lone, dark clouds at the horizon. Then we tried Cornwall. There were four of us by then, me, my sister and our step-siblings, another boy and girl. We played Enid Blyton: four go mad in Cornwall, making up mysteries that didn't exist, imagining smugglers and criminals hidden down among the coves.

There was another holiday camp after that, a fleeting visit with my grandparents to France by car and ferry to a place called Saint-Jean-de-Monts in the Vendée, which I realize now isn't actually that far from the miserable barn I visited with Peter and La near Nantes. When I was little, though, the journey seemed endless, mile after rolling mile of countryside. They were of the generation, my grandparents, who liked a holiday camp, everything laid on. On the upside, the French weren't so big on balloon-dancing: no wonder I fell in love with France, though I do remember a theme park near there called Pepita Park, which looked as if it could have been conceived by David Lynch, or lifted straight out of Stephen King's *It*. I remember it being very empty, and that night had set in. The rides looked skeletal, very rickety, there was a half-moon rising and the air was muggy, then these face painters came loping out of nowhere. I ran, and I remember them chasing me, their faces painted like lions, actors coming out of the darkness and trying to make us jump. That was a lot for a ten-year-old to stomach. Where were the other people? It was like being stuck in a dream.

* * *

The first plane I boarded was to go to Greece with a girlfriend, on a Ceefax holiday. That will probably go over the heads of a lot of people reading this, but Ceefax was like the internet before the internet, coming through your telly in blocky primary colours. The pages took ages to load, but for £110 each, Ceefax got my girlfriend and me to Greece for seven days of island hopping. You'd be hard pushed to Google that nowadays. It was amazingly exciting that first flight. Like a lot of those bargain-bucket trips, take-off was in the wee small hours, and I was still drunk because I hadn't been to bed. We'd stayed up drinking, dreaming of clambering on a flight before sunrise and arriving in Greece, a new, alien world. I'm romanticizing it out of all proportion, but it was my first time in the air. I can't imagine taking that for granted. My hangover was just kicking in as we came in to land, and the pressure on my ears as we descended felt like a spike behind my eye. I remember seriously considering never going home again if that's what you had to contend with on every flight. Oh, to be so innocent . . .

The island hopping was short-lived. We woke up one morning to learn that a ferry had sunk off the island we were staying on, Paros, and watched as all the town's families came out in mourning, and the buildings were swathed in black. Almost everyone there had lost somebody they knew, a relation or friend, and the beautiful, colourful island closed down, the bells stopped ringing, everything stilled. We were marooned, two tourists sticking out like sore thumbs. Nobody paid us any attention, but it suddenly felt very *Wicker Man*. When we finally got a boat out of there we had to sail over the wreckage.

* * *

I'd stopped using Ceefax by the time travel became a big part of my life with the band. Sitting on a bus all locked and loaded and ready to go, on tour with a proper budget and support from your label, was quite a feeling. And a tour bus takes you on a journey to a strange environment. All you see of every town you visit is the bus, the back of the venue and a concentrated adoration in a room. Then there's loads of snogging and whatnot and writing on jeans, everyone's on stage hugging you, and every bit of press you read and every picture you see is of yourself, and you begin to feel like the centre of the universe. It's easy to see how people get remote and arrogant. I'd like to think that we learnt quickly. You do things on your first tour that you never do again, only throw the proverbial TV out of the Travelodge window the once. After you've finished the initial tour, you're kind of over it, you know you're not Keith Richards and so you stop trying to pretend you are. We did manage to get banned from the Ibis in Swansea (I think it was, at least – how rock 'n' roll) on that tour, though we were acting like idiots and I don't blame them.

I first flew with The Libertines to Sweden, and then we rolled through Europe on our own tour bus. It was as if my feet didn't touch the ground, just a succession of wonders. It's hard to explain how exciting your first times abroad on a tour bus are; you really feel like you've stepped up in the world. We were out supporting

Supergrass after our first album, and their crew hated us and their fans hated us, but our record was galloping up the charts for the first time and Europe was rolling through the tour bus window. I'm not sure that I've ever felt so happy or fulfilled. It felt like we were making our mark in the world, planting our flag on the bloody horizon.

People say that if you're touring in a band you don't see places – you know, telling Montreal they've been a great audience when you're actually in Milan – but that's only if you choose not to. I was keen to soak up as much of the atmosphere of all the new places as I could. We always made sure to meet the savviest, nicest, smartest locals, and let them take us on a whistle-stop night out after the gig, or go to somebody's house and party. There were proper adventures everywhere we went. Barcelona and Madrid were particularly cool. We made the video for 'Time For Heroes' in Madrid completely drunk, and there's one bit in there on a metro platform where the train's pulling through the station and I jump against it. I leapt into it, and I could easily have gone between the carriages: I could have died, never been seen again, but I sort of staggered around, dusted myself off, then I was back in the game. That's how we were living; we felt indestructible. The warmth of the people in Spain was amazing – friendly, beautiful people – but we had a great reception the world over. We found the same intimacy with our fans that we'd created in London all over the world, which was a beautiful thing. We effervesced, and the audiences fed on that and the buzz was bounced straight back. We'd arrive at the venues and find fans waiting, ready to embrace the spirit of Libertinism we brought.

* * *

We came back from that first tour more worldly wise, more used to other countries, but nothing we'd met could prepare us for our first visit to Japan. It seemed like a different universe. Our debut offering was out and selling well: we were officially big in Japan (though thankfully no one in the band actually said that out loud) and we'd been booked for a headline tour. The first thing that happened when we landed was that a little dog came and sat down next to me. We'd all been drinking for the duration of the flight, and I thought it was the sweetest thing in the world – one of the special welcome dogs had taken a shine to me. Of course, it was the drugs dog, and they sit next to you to indicate they can smell something on you. There must have been some residue of something or other on my clothes because suddenly I'm off in a room, they've shut and locked the door and they're stripping me down. The speed at which my clothes left my body was jaw-dropping. They sat me at a table in my pants and put a big laminated folder in front of me. Inside, on the first page, there were several pictures of pills, a whole spectrum of uppers and downers that I'd never seen before.

'You have?' asked the customs officer.

'No,' I said.

More pills: 'You have?'

LSD: 'You have?'

Crumbling lumps of hash, mounds and mounds of coke, a page

full of syringes, it goes on for absolutely ages. Then it stops. And they smile, and I smile, and everyone seems pleased. Then the officer interviewing me stands up, slides the folder off the desk, and returns with another one, which he pushes towards me. It's full of pictures of automatic weapons. He starts in again: 'You have?'

During it all, I was absolutely petrified. Even without any illegal drugs or automatic weapons, it was scary simply sitting there in my pants in a foreign country, being questioned by customs officials.

Though my initial welcome could have been better, Japan was a revelation. I can be something of an anorak, so in a new country light years from my own my eyes were popping out of my head at the smallest things. We'd stop at a petrol station, for instance, and I'd be out in the shrubs looking for weird poisonous spiders and things. Admittedly, it's not the way David Attenborough goes about things, and I'm hardly likely to find rare specimens in the road, sadly, but it was all new to me and I wanted to see as much as I possibly could.

It was the little things that were different. We'd cross the road when there was no traffic, as you would in London, and the girls following us around would be in hysterics because we'd crossed the road illegally. And even though we only had one record out, the reception we got was intense, like Beatlemania as soon as we got into town. In fact, we stayed at the Capitol Hotel Tokyu in Tokyo, once, for a festival, which is where the Beatles had stayed, though the original building has now been razed to the ground, and there were different tribes of groupies camping in the lobby around the clock, sort of hissing at each other, quietly hating each other, while they waited. When the band that they were waiting for came down in the lift, they would just shoot up and rush towards them, different sections of the lobby rising up in ordered blocks when the lift doors parted and a band stepped into sight. While we were there, Peter bagged a girl who ended up staying with us for three days. He set her the task of doing his laundry, while we were out playing and doing promo work, and of finding some fighting beetles. I thought the beetles were a stretch, but when he returned to his room the laundry was still in a heap on the floor. As far as we could tell, she'd sat on the bed for three days, watching TV and enjoying room service. She had a nice tour.

By the time we took the famed bullet train, our first Japanese tour was grinding us down. We'd started drinking on the plane out of London and I wasn't sure we'd stopped. Somebody had recommended Berocca to us, so we started overdosing on it, hoping the fizzy coloured water would offset damage we were otherwise doing to our bodies. We were strangely optimistic in this and equally, for all our combined cynicism, the bullet train took our collective breath away. It looked alive even sitting there under the station's blue stone awning, and the glorious engineering would have made Isambard Kingdom Brunel proud. As we glided off into the Japanese countryside, I felt nature call, so I went to find the toilet in the hypermodern train. I arrived at the bathroom to find something resembling the inside of the cockpit of a Formula One car. It was completely incomprehensible. It had a thing shaped like a funnel at one end, and I worked out that you could squat over it and then relieve yourself into what appeared to be an opening. I was very wide of the mark in so many ways. The bright green pee ran down the side of my foot and out under the door. I steadied myself, shook myself off and, embarrassed, spent a little longer than necessary tidying up. As I stepped out of the door, everybody stared at me, as if I was a vigilante walking through the saloon doors in an old western. I hadn't factored in that we were travelling at three hundred miles an hour. The glowing green Berocca piss had gone streaking along the aisle and terrified the entire carriage. I could have had someone's eye out; it was like having a very poor superpower.

Somewhere out on the road, we bought some exotic looking fireworks, but when we got back to the city we realized we had nowhere to set them off. Band logic quickly dictated that they be let off in the hotel room. They made an amazing sound and the colours were quite beautiful, until one of them shot out of the open window and straight into this pond full of koi carp, which are sacred in Japan. There was a godawful sound as the firework fizzed and exploded in the pond, the water boiled and hissed, and all these wonderful looking fish were suddenly still. One by one they began to float, belly up, to the surface. We pressed our faces against the glass and wondered what the sentence was for killing a pond full of protected fish. Then, very slowly, they started moving, stirring a little in the water. The firework had just stunned them, thank God. As my awareness returned to my immediate surroundings, I heard a crackling sound. We turned as one and realized that another errant rocket had got stuck in the ceiling tile, and was happily fizzing away. We hit the floor just as it exploded. We only had a few rockets left, so we thought it a good idea to fire one off along one of the Capitol's very long, straight corridors. As it hared out of sight, a chambermaid stepped into view. She had just enough time to mouth a silent 'oh' before it crashed into the door only feet away.

We stopped lighting fireworks after that and just sat waiting for management to come pounding on our door; but no one ever came. I miss the Capitol.

* * *

Miniatures pile up on your seat-back table, films start and finish, duty free, lights dim as you descend. Luggage carousels revolve, air miles accrue, taxi doors slam. Wake up, sir, please put your seat upright, we're landing. We were out at the Coachella Festival, on our first American trip, and there was already a bit of a problem with the brown. Peter had turned up at the airport with some, which he'd had to flush away before we went through to the gate. I remember he came back and he was looking very red-eyed, and I don't know if that's because he was crying because he'd had to flush his stash, or if he'd taken a little something before we flew. It was an emotional time for us all, and I pretty much sedated myself, too. I'm not a good flyer. I hate the lack of control you have when you're in the air. I'm not sure what I can do about it – it's not as if they're going to let me into the cockpit to take over for a bit – so I have to try hard to zone myself out.

Coachella was a bittersweet experience. We drove out through the desert, and I remember the feeling of the air as we travelled into the night, a heavy, humid blast that buffeted the rustling palms. It was the first time I'd ever felt anything like it. We arrived in Palm Springs, and I was sitting on the veranda, jet-lagged, taking it all in, when the storm broke and the rain belted down into the dust. I awoke the next morning to fresh air, crystal light and a hummingbird floating effortlessly outside my window. I was so excited that I phoned my dad to tell him about it. Well, he said, it's raining here, and I've got to go to work. When we got to the site, it was a completely different world from the Reading Festival or anywhere like that, all movie trailers and Winnebagos, and Cameron Diaz playing crazy golf backstage; for a moment I guess we all thought we were going to Hollywood to be living the life that Russell Brand is now enjoying.

*　*　*

That was a dream that quickly died, as Groove Armada, or whoever it was on stage before us, ran over time, leaving us, as the last band on, no time to play before the strictly enforced lights-out cut-off time. Some of the organizers told us not to, but we went on stage regardless, and about half a song in, they turned all the power off. We carried on playing acoustically in the dark, with thousands of people in front of us singing along. I remember somebody asking me at the time why we didn't just leave, and the answer to that was simple: it was our fucking turn to play. The security guards who came to escort us off were all armed, and I remember we were given another gig the next day to make up for it but, of course, we then created even more of a fucking stir. Suddenly we'd become those bad boys from London again. It was all a long way from the Dublin Castle.

We were painted as hellraisers, and we did have our ponds-full-of-stunned-koi moments, but Coachella was one of only three times I can remember that we were escorted off stage for bad behaviour. Much later, I was kicked off the stage for smoking at the SXSW Festival, playing with Dirty Pretty Things, and the guards there, like at Coachella, were also armed. That should have been no surprise, though – they like their guns in Texas. Another time, at CBGBs in New York, a cigarette got me wrestled off stage – no wonder they say it's bad for you. I was physically dragged off the stage in a headlock with a ciggie in my mouth, off the stage and out the back, and – this will tell you something about The Libertines – the band just kept playing. Thanks, lads. Then I came back on rather sheepishly with a red face and ruffled hair, no cigarette, and carried on, too. David Letterman also told me to put my cigarette out once, just after we did 'I Get Along' on his show. Marilyn Manson, whose real name is Brian, was on, too. We were ordered not to talk to him, but Brian got into the lift with us, so we got out, ran down the stairs and, as the lift doors opened and Brian got out, we were playing and singing 'We'll Meet Again'. He thought it was simply hilarious at the time. He gave us his exasperated face, which I imagine he gives to a lot of people, and just pushed past us. Johnny Knoxville was on, too, but he was smart and handsome, which hurt more than Manson's rebuke.

I had a thing about the Ed Sullivan Theater, where Letterman was being filmed, because it was where The Doors originally sang 'Light My Fire' for Ed Sullivan, and Jim Morrison had refused to change the lyrics, resulting in a lifetime ban from the show. I first fell for The Doors when I was fourteen and a friend gave me a cassette of the first Doors album, a summer otherwise marked by Rage Against the Machine and a school exchange trip to France (the start of another love affair). Fourteen's the perfect age to fall for The Doors: you fail to see the pomposity in the music, and you're not yet cynical about Jim Morrison and how bloated and over the top he would become. I fell for his lyrics, liked how he sounded and how he looked, brooding on the LP covers. Then I heard 'The End' and it scared me a little bit. Years later I watched a buffalo sacrificed and Coppola's jungle burn while that song played and it all made perfect sense: it's the right sound for a world that's coming to an end. Discovering that album at that age chimed perfectly with owning my first guitar, and realizing that I was my own person and not necessarily just a product of my family and upbringing. The magic would wane for me over the years, but I fell for Morrison's lyrics, and, for a while, my interest reached the level of a minor obsession. Later still, I had an ear problem and had to visit a doctor in LA, and the doctor I was sent to, Dr Sugerman, was the brother of Danny Sugerman, The Doors' manager, whose books I'd pored over as a teenager. Doctor Sugerman's waiting room was covered with gold and platinum discs, interspersed with framed black-and-white shots of the good doctor glad-handing the great and the good. It would have been easy to sneer, but I felt my jaw dropping at the sight of Sugerman, MD, pumping Frank Sinatra's fist.

The Doors lead me to Huxley, Huxley to William Blake. I was a sponge soaking it all up. I devoured *Brave New World*, *The Doors of Perception* and *Eyeless in Gaza*, and then collections of Blake's poems, but it was Blake's paintings of heaven and hell that haunted my dreams. I finally got to see some of his work on a day trip to London, off the train at Waterloo, the familiar thrill of the city running through my skinny chest, and up to Trafalgar Square, the pigeons grey blurs against the National Gallery. Inside it was as quiet as a library, the bustle of school parties a distant din, and there were Blake's heavens rent asunder, life and death streaming through. How could you not love that? How could you not be marked forever by it?

But back to LA and Letterman: it meant a lot to me to be there at the Ed Sullivan Theater, preparing myself as best I could to take that stage. Not even The Rolling Stones had followed in Jim's footsteps and stood up there and sworn on TV: Mick was forced to sanitize the lyrics to 'Let's Spend The Night Together', and I thought, before I went on that night, I might be able to make a mark in history, too. In 'I Get Along' I have to say 'Fuck 'em' but, just as we were standing in the wings, the floor manager pulled me aside: 'You're aware there's no swearing, right?' he said. 'Because if you do we're just going to cut it, you're going to look stupid.' I ended up substituting it for 'Your mama', being as it was a Mothers' Day edition of the Letterman show.

Aside from The Doors connection, it had always been an ambition of mine to play a full Broadway 'theater'. And those things, combined with the fact that the performance went out to many millions of people, made it one of the defining moments for me, definitely a high point of The Libertines. For once, it wasn't just about having a riot: we did something that was going to endure. I watch that clip on YouTube every now and again, when I'm drunk, and you can see my fag burning on the drum riser. And, as I go to put it out when we finish, I unintentionally blank David Letterman. I leave him hanging. From seminal rock 'n' roll rebellion through blanking Letterman, to being told off for smoking a fag: oh, the highs and the lows. The Libertines were always a bit like that for me. And I will always enjoy the memory of him telling the audience that we looked like the guys on the Quality Street tin. In our matching red jackets how could we argue?

* * *

Even on later trips to the US, the magic of the place didn't wear off. May 2003: Marilyn Monroe is hanging on the wall in our apartment at the Off Soho Suites on Rivington Street in New York. Like every skinny white boy from the countryside I'd romanticized New York out of all proportion, but having driven into the city, to see downtown laid out before us like a Woody Allen film set, Gershwin trumpeting in my head as the orchestra swelled and steam rose in the city streets, I thought it might fulfil my fantasies like no other destination I'd ever seen. We craned our necks like tourists, taking everything in; then there we were on our own little Manhattan street, in a building where Marilyn had once stayed. What made the dream for me (aside from thinking that Marilyn had slept in my bed, which was, admittedly, unlikely) was the air-con unit, which was of the sort you see rattling away in movies, sticking out of the window, fizzing and dripping icy water onto the carpet. I couldn't have been more in the moment. The first thing I did after I arrived was take a fistful of dollars over to the store to buy Coca-Cola to put in the fridge. It just felt right. We were in New York for press promos and a few live shows at the

Bowery Ballroom, which sold out, and one in Brooklyn at a place called Lux, which barely lasted longer than we did. *Spin* and a few other magazines came to interview us, and the reception was great, but what really elated me was that I felt like I had my own apartment in New York, with a little sofa and a telly, a bed and a kitchenette. The only thing that spoilt it was that I'd picked up a Vanilla Coke by accident, which really pissed me off and ruined everything a little. That's how important it was that the moment was absolutely right. Peter and I had a month to immerse ourselves in the city, and there's a photo of me swinging off a lamp-post on Broadway that for me sums up our optimism. We really felt we could make things happen; but, us being us, being in town for a month simply meant we had plenty of time for things to go really tits up.

There are moments like these in the history of The Libertines when even I can see the car crash coming. It looms so vivid and dense that there's no denying it. Peter was floating away from me and I was there, remote and useless, tethered to the ground. Peter had the brainwave that you could get crack off any homeless person anywhere in New York City. I was trying to point out that, inspired as it was, his thinking was a little flawed, given the situation these people found themselves in. Peter, however, shrugged when I mentioned it and scanned the street for people who looked like piles of old clothes because that was where happiness lay, I suppose, for Peter at that time.

Then there was a girl Peter had met in England before we flew out to the States, one of those ghouls and goblins that he brought flocking out of the shadows. Although she scrubbed up pretty well if she had to, I found her pretty grotesque, given the situation. Naturally, I was delighted when she turned up in New York. She always had a camera with her, filming everything all of the time, always in your face. Later on I realized it was our camera, the band's camera, that she had decided to commandeer after she shacked up with Peter. It started out as a chronicle of our time there, though eventually, inevitably, she simply stole it, which endeared her to me just that little bit more.

In a matter of days, Peter had random homeless guys coming up to our apartment and she's there circling around this camera, filming constantly, whirring away like some fucking vulture. I could feel the whole situation building, my anxiety rising that I was losing Peter, and I just wanted to pull my best friend out of there, and say, 'Look, can we just get on with what we're doing?' We were trying to work on demos, but things eroded and fell apart and I'd lose him, literally; he was just disappearing all the time. One day, I was looking for Peter and I went upstairs to the roof, and the pair of them were up there playing one of my songs that I'd been working on. The girl was making up lyrics, ad-libbing and doing a nauseating freeform dance; then she turned to me and said, 'Peter and I are writing songs, come and join us.' *This has gone very wrong,* I thought, as I imagined pushing her off the roof, her thin frame falling to the street below, still talking all the way down. Instead I said, 'Pete, can I have a word?' But he just ignored me. Not long after, he started not to want to do anything at all. All the obvious symptoms of his drug use were showing themselves.

There was the occasional respite, the sense of trying to claw something back. We got our Libertines tattoos in the city, my spidery handwriting on both our arms in some sort of attempt to bind us together, although we didn't even have them done in the same place. Peter went to Chinatown for his, and I got mine down in the Bowery. And, later, he came to me for help at the apartment when he couldn't clear out the junkies who had gathered in his room. I remember his face at my door. He looked scared, wide-eyed and a bit lost. It had all got a bit hairy by this point: money had started to be owed because he'd go out and meet people to score, then everyone would share and the dealers were putting it all on Peter's tab. It hadn't got heavy, there was no muscle turning up, just these weasel-faced junkies moaning and bitching and doing anything to try and get a hit. For no good reason other than he's my best friend I went down there – while he sat it out in my room – and there were about six of them sitting in a circle with the lights out. It was like going into a squalid cave, and they're just sitting, absolutely useless, wallowing in their own filth. I'd just had it by this point, and, it sounds strange to say, as I told them to get out I felt as if I had a white light around me. It felt like opening the curtains on a summer morning: the light just went through them, these horrible black shadows, and they dispersed. I can't remember if Peter thanked me or not. Let's say he did.

* * *

I'd travelled to New York full of hope, and I was to return home with a heavy, heavy heart. I was realizing that I was at the beginning of the end of my band, my best mate was becoming unreachable and that, though we had the world at our feet, all the things we'd ever dreamed of, we were just pissing all over it, throwing it all away. We were the hot ticket in town, albeit briefly: Damon Albarn turned up to one of our shows, acting oddly, and I remember him telling us to be more horrible to our crowd, that we needed to be nastier to them. One of Bananarama also came by and told me, and this felt like a dream, that we weren't punk, but they, Bananarama, were. Bananarama were punk. I remember someone saying backstage that we'd got some pretty eminent musicians in to see us so we must have been doing something right. We were creating a buzz in New York, we were actually in demand there, and not just with other British bands. It felt that we were on the verge of something big – if we could only keep ourselves together long enough to get there.

* * *

Even after I chucked all of the junkies out for Peter, his days didn't return to normal. He went into lockdown with his girl, and we weren't getting anything done so, eventually, I sort of gave in to it all and turned tourist. I took to the streets, if only to dispel the sick feeling sitting at the base of my stomach. I remember standing on the Staten Island Ferry and taking in the Statue of Liberty in the distance, and travelling to the top of the Empire State Building, looking out over the city and feeling utterly deflated. We'd come all this way, metaphorically and physically, and for what? For my best friend to crouch down in his fucking room with a pipe and a bunch of strangers?

The thin, fragile raft we'd built was starting to take on water, and our beautiful gathering of friends was slowly disintegrating. I've always found it difficult to live in the moment, always been scared about losing what I've got, often to the point of not enjoying it. And now it seemed as if my fears were being realized.

FOUR

Can't Stand Me Now

Another year – 2003 – another NME Awards. This time around they've moved to the Hammersmith Palais, the venue that inspired one of The Clash's greatest songs, a venue that's now been turned into luxury flats – London's good at papering over its own history. We were nominated for Best Newcomer, and I remember being very nervous, even though we'd been told that we'd won already. I knew we had the award in the bag, but, typically, a part of me was telling myself, *No, they're just saying that so we'll turn up, we haven't really won.* Sometimes I'd give anything for my nerves to take a back seat. All the band were there, as well as Irish Paul, who was sitting across from me dressed in military garb. And, to stop my aforementioned nerves having their way with me completely, I was getting very drunk. There were silver buckets filled with booze in the middle of all the tables, which we were doing a good job of emptying, and I remember feeling so proud and scared when our award was announced. We walked up to the stage and, just as we were stepping on to it, Peter turned round and gave me a mocking, horrified look and said, 'What *are* you wearing?'

I had a leather jacket over the top of my suit, which, due to a combination of nerves and booze, I hadn't thought to take off. It was a terrible moment: my dreams were coming true, and being dashed by Peter in exactly the same instant. I still find it hard to say how I felt, but it was crushing, as if he'd just leant over and gobbed in my fucking coffee. I thought he must have done it simply to be nasty and it just totally floored me. While we were getting the award all I felt was twitchy and very self-conscious.

* * *

Regardless of those circumstances, I loved that leather jacket. It was a motorbike jacket that my dad had owned since he was the age I am now, and which at some point along the line he'd managed to dye black from its original red. When we were young my sister wore it to school and then, when she'd had her fill, I inherited it. My dad also owned a guitar, but that I wasn't allowed to touch. It was a prized thing that he didn't want anyone breaking; he didn't like us touching his stuff generally. I understand his attitude, now. Years later I used to be skittish when we were playing at the Albion Rooms and people came careering towards one of my guitars: who wants to own a broken guitar? Even so, when I was a kid I'd still sneak downstairs at night, when the house was quiet and the others were asleep, and I'd practise 'riffs'. I'd feel my way around songs I liked, trying to work out bridges and how the music flowed. I'd practise Nirvana songs: they were pretty simple in their setup and a good place to start, and

I bought a *Hendrix Made Easy* guitar book, which was very weird. In it, all his songs were stripped back to their most basic form, but the thing with Hendrix is that you don't want it to be easy. His songs don't work without his flair, so they just sounded alien and obtuse.

It took me ages to learn to play, much longer than it takes the average person. I taught myself, made myself do it, even though it yielded so little for so long. I had some friends who'd been at it and they were suddenly fluid in a week, bloody junior Eddie Van Halens all of them. Someone once asked me how long it took me to learn, and, without being pat in my response, I told them that I still was learning – I still am. Learning to play guitar filled the space that had grown inside me. I couldn't play enough.

I wasn't just a slow learner at the guitar; girls eluded me, too. My friends were learning fast by the time they were thirteen, but my shyness could be crippling, and I was quite the oddball, the outsider. I had no emotional intelligence whatsoever. I'm not sure if that came from my parents' divorce, but it took me years to bloom, to come into myself. One of my half-brothers had a similar thing, but with a very different upbringing, so it could be that it was a genetic thing. I had a fragility about me that made everything very difficult, but then a liberal mother, and a new home with an extension, opened the world up for me. When my mother moved back to Whitchurch from the communes it was with her new man, a man who more or less became my stepdad. Their liberal attitude (my mother once impressed my mates by showing one of them how to skin up) combined with a wood-and-glass conservatory that they had built on to the back of the house, suddenly meant I could spend hours with my friends, drinking and smoking dope and playing guitar. This helped my social life no end, even made me cool in some people's eyes, and, all the while, I was practising on her new man's guitars. He didn't mind me playing them, and even started to give me some pointers. He was also very encouraging about my playing and about my ambition to get out of town and see the world, to find myself. I'm very indebted to him for that still. I think back now to those summers and my homes either on my dad's estate or in the English countryside with my mother and her friends and I know my parents did the best they could with my sister and me, but we'd both fled a long time before we actually left.

* * *

Back to the jacket, though. Some triple-faced rat nicked it when we were playing a gig in Leeds. Every time I go to Leeds to play now there's a rumour: *I know someone who knows someone who's got your jacket.* It just drives me potty. What I want to say is 'Fuck off', but I desperately want the jacket back. It's the closest thing I've got to a family heirloom. The first few times I was up there and looking for it, I ended up on a stupid wild-goose chase, an utter waste of my time. I'm still really angry about it, which is hardly likely to help my cause or ensure I'll see my jacket any time soon.

It was strange, the cult of The Libertines: it was romance and poetry, a vehicle for this ragtag gang with guitars, something that people often desperately wanted to be a part of. We were the kind of band who let people in. We wanted to pull those barriers down between them and us, and we engaged with our fans, in a true, direct, way, long before such engagement – using the internet and social media – became a tool of the record industry. And I'm not sure if we invited it, or deserved it, but people did take our stuff. It's sad, in a way, but it wasn't ever malicious. They wanted mementos, things like our mobile phones, and really mundane objects: little bits of paper, items of clothing, foreign coins, plectrums, packs of guitar strings; sometimes they took the food on our rider. I enjoyed their enthusiasm, but it wore thin and we quickly realized that there comes a point where there has to be some order. Suddenly we're hungry and we can't make phone calls. Most bands would have thrown their hangers-on out on their ear, but we were trying to prove a point, often haplessly as it turned out.

* * *

It had been quite the turbulent year when we returned to the NME Awards in 2004. That might explain why we were so drunk. However, by then it seemed as if we were always drunk so the reasons behind it were pretty hard to fathom. We were to play 'Don't Look Back Into The Sun' that night, but the reason we sent a ripple through the room was that Peter and I didn't accept our Best British Band award by spouting platitudes or gurning happily into the cameras. Instead, we recited Siegfried Sassoon's war poem, 'Suicide in the Trenches', which had a bit more impact than the usual monkeys thanking their labels, or saying, 'Cheers, yeah', and punching the air.

My relationship with that poem and the way we read it that night began, really, when I was at school, and studying war poetry. Everyone had to read a poem and my nerves were such that, in order to read the passage without having to deal with myself, I played a backing tune then just half sang the words over it instead. It was sort of hillbilly style, and it was actually quite effective; if it sounded comic, then it was only the comedy of nervousness, and it stuck with me. I kept reciting the poem like that for years, and I taught it to Peter. Sometimes when we were warming up we'd play it, just the two of us together.

At the NME Awards, however, even the old routine could not act as a sticking plaster over our differences. There was a lot of tension between us because that time was the beginning of us really falling apart. Peter had wanted to hide in the wings and then bounce out on to the stage, to make a whole 'Where's Peter?' joke to make light of his increasing absences that year. That was what I was prepared for but then he just strolled out on stage and spontaneously started to recite the first line. So I followed with the second and we went from there. I was annoyed at the time, but in retrospect it made sense to me. It's an incredible poem and when we got the final stanza you could see people at the front really listening, eyes wide open:

You smug-faced crowds with kindling eye,
Who cheer when soldier lads march by,
Sneak home and pray you'll never know,
The hell where youth and laughter go.

It caused a stir when we did it, and in the papers the next day, but really it highlighted how incidental and minute what we were actually doing was in the grand scheme of things. And how all of the bullshit, the big balloon of music industry egos, can be burst with a sliver of truth. Then we just walked off, and I'm pleased that we did: it was impossible to follow.

I'm glad it resonated. It was a really important time and place to remember war and sacrifice. Time set aside for remembrance is important, but I think it's much more powerful to recall things like that out of context – it shouldn't just be boxed up and brought out once a year, it should be part of the everyday consciousness. Plus, at those awards, you're in a room full of young men who have no idea what it would've been like to have been that age and in the trenches. It had never occurred to them: they lived in the moment, thought they *were* the moment, and were happy to sit there and pat themselves on the back while getting wrecked on free Monkey Shoulder whisky.

* * *

Our world may have been falling apart, but even that provided inescapable moments. I'll never forget Peter fleeing the stage when we'd sold out three nights at the Brixton Academy. We were playing at a good tilt but our much-touted camaraderie was a sham that night, and underneath we were fighting, fucking it up. Peter and I exchanged glances and then he just took off running. Later he'd tell me that I looked at him funny, and that might have been true, but not enough to cause him to take off into the streets of south London. Our two bodyguards, twin brothers Jeff and Michael, were there in the wings. They'd worked with Biohazard for a while and it showed. Jeff looked a bit like *Popeye*'s Bluto, which I always found

91

quite reassuring for some reason, and they were both stacked, hugely muscular, massive and wide, both tattooed from their necks to their shins. They were from Oxford, and they were very gentlemanly, very proud to be English, a real oasis of calm backstage, sipping their tea. I think their dad is from Africa and their mum's a lovely little Geordie lady who I've met, and they were terrifyingly good at their jobs. They went with me to Dirty Pretty Things for a while, mainly because I liked having them around.

Jeff and Michael were a great wall between Peter and the world, such an immediate deterrent that usually people didn't even try to get close. They were incredibly quick, too: more than once someone lunged for Peter (and I include myself in that, but they didn't try and stop me, thankfully; it would have been like seeing a big dog wrestle a chew-toy), and on one occasion when somebody had a half-hearted go at him, one of the brothers just shot out this mighty fist and, though it was genuinely a blur, it seemed to land almost gently, more like a push, and this guy just went up in the air and over like a well-struck skittle. It was incredible.

So Peter was running headlong into the backstreets of Brixton, all churning legs and porkpie hat, and his security was chasing after him, which must have dazed passers-by, like seeing lights in the sky you can't explain. I've no idea where Peter was going, I doubt he did either, and they rounded a corner and some skanky crackhead, who must have thought Peter had robbed a shop, stuck his foot out, to try to trip Jeff up – honour among thieves and all that – and Jeff, without breaking his stride, gave him a little body check and bounced him off about three walls. I bet he didn't know what hit him. Literally. It was strange, though: there was no malice or premeditation. Jeff was just protecting his charge. In Peter's case there was a lot of protecting to do.

While Jeff and Peter were doing circuits of south London's least salubrious neighbourhood and the crackhead was rolling around in the gutter, we, the remaining Libertines, were debating going back on stage. We were getting increasingly used to making shitty, agonizing decisions such as whether to go back on stage a man down or not. Even if he had run off, and was disappearing more and more, Peter was still an integral part of the band. Eventually, we decided to get it together and go back on, reasoning that the gig was sold out and that, until Peter scarpered, we were having a suitable degree of fun. Back on stage, we were playing the songs, hoping the audience was appreciating what we were doing, and how difficult it must have been for us, and suddenly there was this big roar. We were made up. Then I turn around and Peter's back on stage. He must have tired himself out running – we were hardly in our prime physically – then heard over Jeff's radio that we were about to go back on and decided that he wanted to be there, too. I was pretty crestfallen if I'm honest. There we were, trying to hold it all together, maintain what little dignity The Libertines had left, and the biggest cheer of the night is Peter deigning to come back and play with us. Someone told me later that they thought it was funny, but it wasn't funny.

When Peter disappeared, most times we bore the brunt of it,

were blamed as if we'd tied him up and locked him in his bunk, as if we were the ones who wouldn't let him join us on stage. Later, I'd insist he left the band for a while in a wretched attempt to save us, but before then we'd have to troop on without him, guessing at where he might be. John and Gary locked into place, me out at the front alone. We got chased out of one gig in Spain because we were a man light. By that stage in the band, we'd factored in that this might happen, and we'd employed a guitar tech who we knew could play and we told him to learn a few of the songs. I think our survival instincts were kicking in. Nick was from Clacton-on-Sea, and he was very much a Clacton-on-Sea boy. Fish and chips and pills; pills and fish and chips. We rather liked him. Then, sure enough, Peter didn't come and I remember being petrified going round Spain. I felt as if I was carrying the weight of the world as we travelled through these little towns, and then came that show where they literally chased us into the street. The new guitar player could only play six songs, and I was too scared to perform up there on my own – it just wasn't an option – and so the crowd began to boo us. We left the stage, were packing up to leave, and there was what pretty much amounted to a lynch mob waiting for us after the gig out at the back of the venue. They looked mad as hell, ready for serious violence, and I had to pacify them – my heart beating out of my chest – by playing our songs on an acoustic guitar standing out there in the street. They were like a football crowd, pushing up in my face, goading and shouting, until their fury began slowly to flatten out, and turn to enjoyment. It changed from being booed and chased out of the venue by a screaming, spitting mob angry at being ripped off, to the same mob telling us what a really special thing we'd done. And, when it had all calmed down, they asked us quite sincerely what we'd done to Peter, as if we'd chosen to take our life in our hands and play with a roadie in his stead. It felt like they thought that if they asked enough times I'd bring him out from behind the bus to rapturous applause, like some magician unveiling his latest trick. It was so sad: people really liked us, and the album was doing plenty of business, but during those gigs in Spain without Peter we didn't have a future.

I never got past being terrified about being on stage in The Libertines without Peter. I needed him on stage with me, missed the physical aspect of it, the charging into each other, having that second voice, that person you could fall back on. I was just so miserable touring without him, and felt duty bound to feel that way because all I was getting, all I was seeing, were the super-fans at the front, the ones who came to fill my brain with questions before the gig. It wasn't their fault, but they didn't have a clue what was going on. When I got off the bus they'd be there, at the venue they'd be there, and I was scared, ashamed and guilty, when I hadn't actually done anything. I was fighting to make it work, paper over the cracks and do the right thing by holding it together. But I would barely have stepped off the bus and someone would ask, 'Why have you kicked Pete out?' You should do this and you should do that. You should give him a second chance.

* * *

It was odd that, even though we were suffering the slings and bloody arrows, we were actually getting really good as a band around that time, and especially when Anthony Rossomando joined. I mean no disrespect to Nick, but Anthony was one of us, and it felt more like a gang again when he came along. I'd had to go to New York to find him, because we needed an American, or someone who could work in America, for our US shows. Three people showed up, two of whom were absolute fruit loops. One started crying before he'd even played; the other was a ginger chap, who said he'd do it but actually seemed reluctant even to pick up the guitar. Then he said he could only play 'math guitar', so I asked him to show me what math guitar was, and he started diddling around on the fretboard. I began to lose the will to live. Neither of them knew any of the songs I'd asked them to audition with; I don't think they even knew who or what The Libertines were, so by the time Anthony came in I didn't care.

'You just play the song, I'm going to play the drums,' I said, though I can't actually play the drums to save my life. Nevertheless, we jammed like that for a while, and I thought, *This is actually working*. Then Anthony switched over to play the drums and a deep friendship was born. As with any audition I've ever done, there was only one real contender, though I do still wonder what the other two guys are doing now.

Anthony, known to many as Stan, is tall and slender, spidery and louche, with a classic Italian American pallor. He became a good sidekick through troubled times, ever willing to defend me in my absence or contest me in my presence. He was part of the band for some pretty memorable gigs, including one with Primal Scream on the support bill in an enormous aerodrome near São Paulo. Our luxury hotel in the city was an island of international money set on a building site, in its own compound, the abutting poverty kept at bay by high fences and bulldozers. We weren't looking out of the window, though: we'd worked out from the menu that the mini-bar's entire contents came to something like two quid, so we cleared it out in twenty minutes – it was as if we'd never seen a half-bottle of wine before. I think we failed to notice the irony that we'd been talking about the plight of the country's poor mere moments before. Gunshots rang out all night, but we paid them no heed. We could barely even speak, so off our faces were we on the local produce. After the gig, we got back to our dressing room and some poor women had made masses of food, like a wedding spread, the centrepiece being a great tower block of sandwiches, made out of bread coloured and shaped into the Brazilian flag. And it was all a little bit dry because it had been out for a while, but because of the state we were in none of us could eat a thing; we felt so guilty about the waste, given the poverty around us, and unpatriotic, but there was nothing we could do.

I'd been to Brazil before with The Libertines, staying and playing in Rio near Copacabana Beach. I remember John attempting to cross the beach to get a hamburger – we were playing football near there, just next to the hotel – and he was about to walk over when a guy in the hamburger stall says: 'No, no, no, they will cut your throat!' We thought maybe he was playing with us, these lobster-pink English boys obviously a bit out of their depth, but only for a brief moment. We caught his eye and you could see he wasn't kidding at all. Suddenly, I felt cold, the kind of chill you can take into a hot shower and you still can't shift.

* * *

I can't pretend I didn't miss Peter, and the band was never going to feel the same, but after Anthony joined I actually managed to enjoy a few shows. I liked Glastonbury, because my mum was there and we were on one of the main stages, and we did a Forum show where Noel Gallagher came and said he liked it. I should qualify that: he was said to have been there and liked it, but I grabbed on to that with both hands, regardless. It helped me to realize that if the crowd are chanting things like 'We want Pete' it helps not to get miserable and feel ashamed, as if it's your fault Peter's not there. I wasn't the one who'd let them down. And, later on, people knew what they were getting when they bought the tickets. Why come if it isn't what you want to see? It made no sense. Fair enough, if you were expecting Jefferson Airplane and you got us. I'd have started chanting then, too, and probably rounded up my own lynch mob and chased myself out into the street. Facing a crowd shouting 'We want Pete' made being on stage an uncomfortable, sometimes horrific place to be. Given that I was trying to hold things together for the fans, it was becoming increasingly hard not to think, *Why am I bothering?* I wanted Pete, too. Yet our options were narrowing until there seemed only one way out.

FIVE

Montmartre

I was standing in Montmartre, underneath the huge white dome of the Sacré-Coeur basilica, and I was telling Peter I didn't want him to come and play with us. I gazed over Paris, over some of the most beautiful architecture I've ever laid eyes on, and I could feel that I was breaking my own heart. From what I could hear over the phone, Peter's heart was breaking, too. He was in Kentish Town, throwing himself at passing cabs and into shop windows, just smashing himself up. *How had it got to this?* I reflected. Peter had failed to turn up for the tour and then there was a will-he-won't-he moment, but in the end we'd made the decision that, for his own sake and ours, at least in the short term, he needed to be out of the band. Something died for me on the hill of Montmartre that day, though it hasn't destroyed my love of Paris, or of France. After visiting the Vendée with my grandparents as a kid, I returned to France at fourteen, ostensibly as an exchange student to learn the language, though it was the thought of getting off with French girls that was driving me at the time. I was a bundle of hormones cased in a prickly skin.

The next time I crossed the Channel – my third ever trip to France – I found myself in Paris, and in Montmartre, for the first time. I'd had an eventful first night in the City of Lights; now, on my second, I was preparing to bed down in the street. I'd run out of money and had nowhere to go, so I made myself into a ball in a futile attempt to ward off the freezing night. Above me Sacré-Coeur in all its luminescent glory, below me the lights of downtown Paris. All I could hear was the sound of my teeth chattering and the whistling of a wind best described as cruel, and thought that now I'd been down and out in Paris and London I could justifiably claim one point of reference with George Orwell. It was cold comfort at best, and I began to picture Rose's Café, a greasy spoon on Bermondsey High Street, where the lights glowed warmly and the door tinkled whenever it was opened. I could smell the bacon and feel a mug of tea in my hands as I opened one eye and pulled my coat tightly around myself. Paris was still there, standing defiantly before me, reaching towards the horizon. I sat up and shivered and lit my last cigarette. I felt like I was out there alone against the universe, but somehow I felt safe.

I'd been working in the Haymarket Theatre as an usher, sleeping on other people's floors and occasionally out on the streets. It's the lowest feeling, getting to the end of the day and having absolutely nowhere to go. No mates to crash out with and you can't go back to your parents because that means you're a complete and utter failure. I remember one night near Hoxton Square attempting to bed down behind some bins, though bedding down without an actual bed is a bit of an anomaly. The Eurostar had just begun operating out of London and they'd been giving away promotional tickets in the *Evening Standard*. Someone I worked with at the Haymarket had won a pair and offered them to me, and my thinking was, *Well, I'm homeless here; I may as well be homeless there instead.* I took my friend Phil, scraping together enough money for one night in a hotel even though we were staying in Paris for two. The hotel room provided a single bed for the two of us, but then I met a girl and Phil didn't. I suggested to him that he give up the bed for the night so that my new female friend could stay – a brilliant idea to my mind, though the look Phil gave me suggested he thought otherwise. We had a minor stand-off at the top of the stairs and then my new friend and I took off on an adventure. I can still see us with our hands linked running into the Parisian night. I'm nothing if not a slightly clichéd romantic, even in retrospect.

That night moved quickly, a brilliant blur. We met dozens of people and, as everyone else faded away, she said she wouldn't give herself to me without protection – which only added to my illusion that I was playing a part on a grand Parisian film set and my life was a movie. Off we went, two would-be lovers with no money trying to blag a free condom. I've touted lone cigarettes a hundred times, but trying to raise a prophylactic is a whole other ball game, if you'll excuse the pun. Eventually, after a fruitless search, she decided to go home and I walked with her to an alien neighbourhood. It was late as she slipped through the door and suddenly there was a lot of shouting coming through the walls, absolute uproar, and I heard heavy footfalls coming down towards me. I turned and ran hard down the street, did a quick left and right and stood panting in an alleyway trying to stop my heart hammering, worried that it would somehow be heard by my pursuers. There was a sliver of starlight above me visible through the buildings and when I stepped back into the small, cobbled street I realized I was hopelessly lost.

I took off in a randomly selected direction, wandering around trying to find my bearings, and I was stealing fruit from outside a corner shop when I reached around into my pocket and discovered I'd lost my passport. My stomach flipped over and I dropped to my knees and squatted there, wishing myself home, wishing that such a place even existed. After a moment, I got up again and began to try to retrace my steps. I figured out roughly where I was, and decided to head for the hot-air risers from the Metro, where all the city's tramps congregate to sleep. There I met a French American, a hulking black guy who was truly out there. I was impressionable and young and open to the idea of meeting new people, new characters, and he was straight out of *Full Metal Jacket*. He kept saying things like, 'They're just sleeping out here, it's like 'Nam!' and I was entranced, but still had the deeply niggling fear about my passport and had no idea where Phil was either. Then, huddled in the warm, musty air stream, I remembered a park that I'd found absurdly romantic, where the girl and I had sat on a bench kissing. Somehow, I made my way back to it, but the quiet of the place had been shattered. The park was filled with raucous Algerian teenagers, who were shouting and hitting each other, and couldn't have been more intimidating to a drunk, confused Englishman. As if on cue, the heavens opened and my trainers, which I'd stolen from a lifeguard at the ponds on Hampstead Heath, slowly filled with rain. The kids had graduated to trying to smash bottles on each other, so I stood there, behind some rather lofty wrought-iron railings, with a fleur-de-lis motif at the top, watching, with rain dripping down my face. Eventually they opened a few bottles of beer, and it was like mother's milk to them. They instantly settled down and moved away from the bench where I'd been sitting earlier. And then I saw it, my passport, there on the bench, almost glowing in the gloom, five hours after I'd unwittingly left it on that spot. It was moments before daybreak, and suddenly it seemed important to get to it quickly, before it got too light and something bad happened, so I clambered over the fence, slipped and fell, and caught my trainer on one of the fleur-de-lis flourishes. I threw out my hands to save myself, straight into a puddle of piss, and so I hung there upside down, inert and stinking of piss, with a stolen trainer the only thing keeping me from cracking my head open, thinking: *What the fuck am I doing?* Somehow, I managed to get down, grab the passport and clear the railings again without either falling in dog shit or suspending myself like a *piñata*. Then I managed to find Phil, too, and, with a few hours still paid for at our hotel, I flopped down on to that single bed. It felt like feather-down pillows and a dozen quilts. I didn't deserve it, but for the rest of that morning I slept the sleep of the just.

* * *

Later on, Peter and I went back to Paris in an attempt to write some songs. It was where, in fact, we wrote 'Don't Look Back Into The Sun'. We hired a flat opposite Sacré-Coeur, which I felt, having roughed it there a few years before, was somehow fitting. The girl who rented us the place worked at PIAS, and she took it all very seriously. She gave us a printed inventory, made us sign some forms and took a deposit, too, and became very irate when, checking the inventory when we left, she found six spoons missing (you might well imagine where they'd got to), though she's now a good friend. We had some fine times there. I remember promising Peter that I could cook and going off to the market to buy the ingredients for bangers and mash. That idea's obviously a non-starter in France, but I was a naïve English idiot. To compound things, I can't cook anyway, a fact that was borne out by the potatoes I eventually served, which were so rock hard that we ended up lobbing them from our balcony at passing tourists.

During that trip Peter decided to get on a train for Italy to catch up with an ex-girlfriend and, no matter how much I pleaded with him not to go, and to stay and write some songs, he went. I was left there alone in the apartment. It wasn't a good time for me to be on my own, and I began to feel utterly lost. Things weren't working out the way I thought they might between us, or with the band, and I was fighting low feelings a lot of the time. With Peter away, the malaise manifested itself in a recurring nightmare in which nightly I tied a rope around my neck and jumped off the balcony to hang myself. I'd wake up each morning, shaken, and the first thing I'd see would be the balcony. Thankfully, a family crisis meant I had to go back to

London and my dreams of hanging above Montmartre stopped.

Perhaps Montmartre, however much I love it, will always be associated with death for me. That day, after I asked Peter not to come and play, I turned my phone off, leaving him to his tempestuous cannonball run across London, and stood there looking out across Paris thinking: *How in the hell are we going to do a gig without him?* My world had been torn apart. He was my best friend and it felt like I'd thrown him away, but it was the only way I knew how to save him. I'm still not sure if I did or not.

*   *   *

I think what killed the band for me was when Peter, the one I knew, my friend, disappeared. At a young age someone in my extended family died from what I now realize was smack, so I figured out pretty early on what hard drugs could do to people, or what people using hard drugs could do to themselves. It stayed with me: if you take heroin you're jumping on board someone else's story and there are only two endings – death or a really fucking boring struggle. I tried to protect Peter from it as best I could, but I suppose he confused smack with the opium ideal of dining on honeydew, finding a gateway to paradise. He disappeared down that tunnel, his sense of humour departed him and he started exploring violence and the horrid things you can do to people. He was razor-sharp, and there was a lot of him. One of the other things I loved very dearly about him was the strength of his convictions: how when he believes in something he won't let it go, no matter how seemingly trivial or illogical it is. If someone tied him down and held a razor blade over his eye and tried to make him renounce something he believed in, then he'd give up that eye. Both his humour and his convictions got lost in the smoke from his fucking crack pipe. And, it seemed to me, he was losing himself, too. After a while, I couldn't bear it.

I often think about that sense of humour, and those young boys with their hopes and dreams who set out together, who had the ability to laugh at themselves, with real humility. I remember once doing a load-in at the Leadmill in Sheffield, and being helped out by a certain woman who still works there now. We opened the back doors of our stinky old van and watched, all five of us, as a pair of pants floated down from the top of a pile somewhere, landing in plain view on an amp. They were blue and inside out, the sort of pants you might see someone wearing in a sitcom, and they had a stain right across them. Most of us started falling about laughing – it being both more embarrassing and more funny because a woman we liked was there – but Peter's face had turned crimson, and quick as a whippet he grabbed the offending briefs and flung them over the yard into a building site next door. I always imagined some brickie walking past and Peter's pants parachuting gently on to his head – because they had to be his: you don't touch someone else's pants, do you? It's not the pants that, for me, make that story precious. It's the humour and the embarrassment, the humility and the humanness of it all, the slapstick moment of a young band out on the make. That was what we lost. The little things that all bands go through like that, things that, when you've been touring for weeks on end in a stinky van full of sweat, don't matter, because you've all set out together to make something whole. Thanks to that togetherness, we became more than the sum of our parts; but when one part fails, it infects the whole thing. Our group of friends, our 'doing it for the Albion', one-for-all spirit, disintegrated, and we became the band you read about in the papers. I think Pete wanted everyone in the band to be sharp and witty all the time, like four would-be Oscar Wildes. But that isn't how everyone is, that's not their vision sometimes.

When we were in the studio making the second album and Alan McGee had hired Jeff and Michael, to keep us from tearing each other's heads off and to stop Peter's ghouls getting through the door, I used to think back to us in the back of that van, and Peter's mysterious pants appearing from nowhere. Later, after I'd had to go on without Peter, I kept my security guard and he protected me from the hangers-on and distressed fans, all of whom wanted to direct their fury and sadness at me. But it was hard to take on other people's misery when Peter left the band, because he'd spread enough of it around already. I'd just try to put myself back on the Staten Island Ferry looking up at the Statue of Liberty, or in that room full of ghosts in our New York apartment block, or on the steps of Sacré-Coeur gazing at the pinpricked sky above Paris, and wonder again where my best friend had gone.

All these places across the world, with the traces of Peter and me running through them, stick in my mind. Paris and France are bittersweet to me now but I keep going back, and even though it's three hours away I can be transported in an instant. It hasn't lost its magic. History still lives in those streets, and Paris has that special thing Manhattan also has – that enigmatic feel. I know the accordion players are only there for the tourists, but I still love hearing their sound filling the air. There's a scene in the film *Moulin Rouge* where you first see Paris, an unrivalled kingdom brimming with magic and possibilities. Romantic that I am, that's how I see it, too. I'll stand on Sacré-Coeur and stare out at the city at night and it will blink its welcome back at me. I'm sure that's what it's saying.

* * *

Life after Montmartre, after The Libertines, gave me ample opportunity to think about fame, and what it had meant to me, and to us, as a band. The first time I ever experienced fame, I think, was when I first came up from the country and into Waterloo Station, the gateway to my dreams, and I bumped into Brian Blessed on the concourse. He was the first famous person I'd ever met, and I was literally dumbfounded. He caught me staring and shook my hand, and the shock of it was so emphatic that it shot up my arm and I thought my head was going to pop off when it got to my shoulder. 'Be lucky!' he bellowed, and I could feel the parting in my hair changing as he said it. It was like being in a friendly wind tunnel. I was elated and Brian grinned. He'd given me something but I'd taken nothing from him, and then we both walked away. And a modest level of fame, when it later came my way, brought me countless untold good things – a pig's heart, for example, at the St John restaurant in Spitalfields, the waiter tapping me on the shoulder, delivering a steaming heart on a plate with a covert salute, a nod of thanks from the chef. It also brought me a drink with Slash at a corporate party. Red Bull were pulling out all the stops: there was a Formula One racing car in one corner and Slash playing guitar in the other; between them, a lush carpet covered with models. The Red Bull was being mixed with vodka, and I sat up at the bar and tried to remember the hows and whys of my arrival at this place, before deciding that neither was especially important. Slash was soloing madly, while his wife danced by his side, playing along to Guns N' Roses songs, and I was so happy to see him and his trademark top hat – even more so when he invited me to his dressing room to tell me what exactly he liked about The Libertines. We sat there wreathed in cigarette smoke chatting, and I tried to hold on to the moment. Three months later, I was walking through LAX, the movie quality light only half softened by the shaded glass that encases the building. Across its concourse I could make out a very familiar figure struggling with a bag and guitar case, a hazy silhouette easily identifiable by the mass of curls and aviator sunglasses sitting halfway down his nose. I strode right up and thrust out my hand. Slash didn't have a clue who I was. He regarded me coolly, like I'd just turned up on the sole of his cowboy boot, and then turned on his heel. He couldn't give me what he thought I wanted or needed.

Notoriety puts you in a bubble, but you can decide how thick the bubble's membrane is. Slash's had become thick enough to protect him, but The Libertines' skin was as thin as a snake's. I'm quiet as a person and The Libertines attracted a hardcore crowd. I always felt I owed them, the ones at the front at least, owed them something I could never quantify but which left me indebted. I'd wanted to take the walls down between us, wanted them in on it, especially live: I had no illusions that I was anything more than the people who were coming to see us. But then, if we'd had a rude audience, people rushed the stage at an inopportune moment or knocked the guitar way out of tune, I'd get pissed off. Contrariness personified, I wanted the intimacy and the frenzy of the moment, but I also wanted my effects pedals to stay where they were and for my lead to stay plugged in. It got contrived later on – the sharing of the space – but the initial rush was incomparable, even if you did slightly fear for your life and occasionally find yourself caught in a headlock by a ginger Glaswegian girl. Even if you had strange hands in every orifice, you had that togetherness, no matter how fleeting.

In the end, our bubble was too thin. Imagined familiarity also breeds contempt, peanuts thrown at my head as a way of saying hello. People telling me my band 'suck', or that I've made a terrible mistake and the first thing I need to do is get back together with Pete, like, right now. For some, there was a tiered system of respect. Sometimes I'd meet blokes who had been in prison with Peter and they'd instantly put their arm around me, their faces close to mine, acting according to an unspoken code: *I did time with Pete, right, I've got this, so I'm worth a good fifteen minutes and all these people here might as well fucking splash on the floor like water.* Or there are boys wanting to kiss you on the lips, which is just a little bit odd – and thankfully there's very little crossover between those two groups.

I remember once standing in the street with a girlfriend, and we're fighting. I know we're breaking up and she knows we're breaking up; she's crying, I'm flushed red in the face and angry, angry and disappointed. Our voices are breaking, we're pulling at each other like two people who are surely going under for the final time. Hoarse and red-eyed, on a quiet, dark street in north London, and then someone taps me aggressively on the shoulder. The only sounds in the street up until then had been us, a sound you'd go out of your way to avoid. 'Hello mate,' he says. Then he says something that, given the context of our meeting, surprises me. 'Mate, I love your band.' He keeps a hold of my upper arm and my soon to be ex-girlfriend and I consider each other quizzically. I'm confused and angry, he's oblivious, happily so. I pull my arm angrily away and then it dawns on him that we might be annoyed with the intrusion. His reaction still makes me furious to this day; I can feel my face going red with rage. 'Well, if that's how you treat your fans!' He stalks off glaring angrily back. I want to ask him if he was a fan, if he cared, then why didn't he ask how we were, what was tearing us apart. My girlfriend catches my eye and then my hand and we trudge solemnly home.

Unlike Liam, the Devil's dick, who, for better or worse, graciously declined my offer in the Dublin Castle to come home and jam with me, I have accepted offers to go to some kid's party, random invitations to someone's house, and I have played many people songs in their own front rooms, and it has been fantastic. But that song is never the end, it's only the beginning. No one ever says after one song, 'That was lovely, thank you, goodbye.' They want more and more: they want to hang out; they want the impact of instant friendship. And I can't give them that. The ones who want to say they enjoy our music, shake my hand and walk off, that I can help with, that I can give them; but some people don't know when to stop and I don't know where to start. I've never been great at drawing lines.

With The Libertines, none of us had really wanted to recreate the kind of fame I'd seen acted out on festival stages – we were never going to be some sort of golden gods – and we hadn't wanted a barrier between us. I don't blame people for doing what they do, whether it's the *NME* reader or the ex-con with a sheen of sweat and wired eyes, but in the end, for us, as The Libertines, it didn't work; it just didn't work. We were sailing to Arcadia, and, to be fair, Peter and I scuttled the ship ourselves. But we were sitting low in the water thanks to all the passengers we'd taken on, and sank all the faster for it.

SIX

Dirty Pretty Things

I wasn't sure what I was hanging on to as The Libertines fell apart, what piece of flotsam or jetsam I'd clung on to as the ship went down. I was out there on my own for a while, but once I'd had time to think about everything I realized that being in a band wasn't out of my system. I began to feel that The Libertines' demise had been a tragedy, because we'd had so much more to say. It also seemed a natural progression, really, because Anthony Rossomando had come into my life during the later stages of The Libertines, and we both felt a creative partnership that had more to give. On a more selfish level, I'd become rather accustomed to the way I was living. There was an element of everyone panicking: *Is this over and, if it is, what are we going to do? God forbid we might have to get real jobs.*

Over many drunken and drugged nights I'd be the reassuring hand on the tiller. *Don't worry, boys, I'll look after you, I'll sort it all out.* Ludicrous coke talk, too many cocktails fuelling my after-hours' bravado. After a while we just assumed this was what we'd do: we'd move on into a new band, and then there was a sudden rush of business and it began to happen. I remember we had a ludicrously long list of band names that everyone had come up with, and frequent pub meetings where we'd verbally tussle over what to call ourselves. It was around that time that John, The Libertines' bass player, quietly left, to concentrate on his band, Yeti, which had previously been a side project. It wasn't a surprise, but it left me feeling deflated all the same. I wish I could tell you that we had a grand plan after that, but if you've read this far then you'll understand that was never going to be the case. We honestly didn't have a clue who might play bass, but we had impetus and we had forward motion: it seemed inevitable that we'd pick someone up along the way. I mean, what's a band without a bass player?

Between bands, I was doing DJ sets to keep my hand in, and I remember playing a festival in Wales called Wakestock, and watching the sun come up over the Welsh coastline after a long, long night. I was sitting on the roof rack of someone's Land Rover with Didz, from Cooper Temple Clause, and playing him two new songs I'd written after The Libertines, the two 'dead' songs, as I'd come to call them. One was 'Bang Bang You're Dead', the other a tune called 'Deadwood' – both destined to be singles, and both reliant on the word 'dead', which later seemed significant. I'd written them on the tide of emotion I was riding coming out of The Libertines, and, in hindsight, they're kind of Libertinesque, but that's where I was, and it was a dark and confused time. I asked Didz what he thought, fishing to see if he'd join the band – as if I was auditioning for him, rather than him auditioning for me. He liked them, and said yes. Anthony was already in, as was Gary, and so we were complete. I'm not particularly proud of poaching Didz from Cooper Temple Clause. I'd met him on the circuit and decided, when we were clear-headed enough to think, that we shared a similar mindset. It felt to me like we pulled him clear of his craft just as it went under, which was sad; I always liked Cooper Temple Clause. But once Didz was in place, we set to work on a new order, our new way, as it were.

This rebirth of sorts was happening right there in Waterloo. I was living near Waterloo Station at the time, and we'd been rehearsing at Alaska Studios, which I think the Slits were involved with in the seventies. We liked its charms and it was next to a gay sauna called the Pleasure Drome, tucked away under the railway tracks, which also added to the whole thing. There was a slightly sleazy feel matched with true endeavour: it felt right. We'd have drunken running races on the South Bank, dashing up and down the paving slabs, being quite competitive about the whole thing, and then go out in the evening to experience the lost pleasures of an innocent night out with friends who you happen to play music with – as opposed to being in clubs and backstage and doing drugs and all of that bullshit. That hadn't happened in a long time, and it seemed so fresh, like a new dawn. We were a very social band, Didz once said to me; and that, when things were going our way, it seemed we didn't have to do much more than walk into a newsagent and it felt somehow significant. At the end of each recording day, we'd go to stand on Waterloo Bridge and look out. Over to the west, the old world and the old order; then, looking in the other direction, to the east, and we could see change coming, strung out under giant cranes. The new world was crouched there, waiting. It's so enigmatic and it's no mistake that Ray Davies chose that sunset to sing about. At the time, too, Waterloo was where the Eurostar came in – or, more importantly, where it could whisk me away to my beloved Paris. I couldn't have really called our first album anything but *Waterloo To Anywhere*. It hinted at my new beginning: free from restrictions, I could literally go where I wanted.

Even before the band was formed, or had a name, I'd already secured us a deal with Vertigo, who had given me *carte blanche* creatively just so they might see what I came up with. And although, suddenly, there were deadlines, deadlines and more deadlines once again, it felt great to be signed to a major. There was a whole unit behind us – video commissioners, A&R, security, cars – and I had a real feeling of creative potential and freedom. The instantaneous upside of the new project was that it felt great to be in a band again, and to have nothing to be apologetic about. I'd loved most of my time in The Libertines, but it had got so tiresome, always having to say sorry for things that I didn't want or were out of my control. With the new band it felt as if we were all on the same page and fighting a good fight. We'd all been in bands before, and tasted some success, and we'd quickly formed a tight unit. We were four people against a world, had our eyes on the prize, and, this time, it felt as if we knew how to get it. In comparison to those early Libertines sessions with Bernard, the first Dirty Pretty Things record was a bit of a breeze: the gang mentality and the adventure were both there. I think for Didz it was a step up from the level he was on, from the way he'd been used to doing things. That's no slight, and, if he'd often seemed surprised by how quickly things were moving, then so were we, but we'd learnt not to show it. We travelled to LA and did the first half of the album with Dave Sardy, who was major league – he's worked with everyone from Marilyn Manson and the Chili Peppers to Johnny Cash. I think someone at Vertigo had decided that there was potential for it to go global, that I could be a singer without borders, if you like, so there was a lot of money being thrown at that first album. It was exciting, the belief that people had in my new band and me, and part of us wanted that recognition. Everyone wants the world to love their record and connect with what they're saying. Alas, it wasn't really to be, but a certain cultish underground did connect with it.

I felt vindicated doing things on my own, and especially as it was around that time that Peter was barely out of the papers and the whole Kate Moss circus was happening. That was always going to eclipse what I was doing, and I wasn't setting out to create chart hits. Peter was better at fame than me: always was, always will be. He dresses and acts the part, he invites the limelight. I sort of admire him for that. I remember playing with Dirty Pretty Things at an old theatre, like the inside of a chocolate box, in Paris, probably towards the end of the band, towards the end of everything. Peter was in the city, and we still weren't properly talking to each other, but, like a lot of estranged 'couples', we were texting. He texted to say he wanted to come to the show and, naturally, I panicked, scanning our set list to see what Libertines songs we were doing. 'I Get Along' was in the running order, and all through the show I was searching the crowd for him, while giving it all I had. He'd never seen us before and I was incredibly nervous. I wanted to make an impression. He was up in the Royal Box, which was exactly the place where I should have thought to look for him, of course. When it came to the last song, we announced that we would love Peter to join us to play 'I Get Along'. The place went absolutely mental, and then there was a long, unwinding moment when it transpired that Peter had left the venue five minutes before, which was both embarrassing and confusing.

* * *

But back to the first album. I'm still proud of that record; it really does capture a time in my life. I think any record should be a snapshot of the time, and, for me, the success, or lack of it, of any of my records is down to their ability to capture a moment, to be a true portrayal of a place in time. The first album broke commercially too, and even if the second one fared less well – and it did – it was true to the time and I wouldn't have it any other way.

In LA, with Dave Sardy, we actually only recorded six tracks, because that's all we agreed to pay for. Dave was pretty strict about that sort of thing. You'd be thinking about recording a seventh song and he'd say, 'It'll cost you ten grand for me to hit the space bar on my computer. Do you want to pay that?' Cue an uneasy air and a nagging voice in my head: *So that's how you want to do it, is it?* It concentrated the mind, all right. We were feeling good and ready to go again that day, but that really put the tin hat on things. We'd spent $70,000 on six songs, so we decided to head home and finish up the rest of them in Glasgow with Tony Doogan. With Sardy we'd all lived on Sunset and Vine in apartments for a month or two. In Glasgow, right at the other end of the rolling-surf-and-swaying-palm-trees spectrum, we rented a big old townhouse right in the middle of the city, but the recording carried on almost seamlessly and Tony did a great job. He perfectly matched the existing sound of the album. I like the way two worlds quietly collide on that one record.

Through all the rehearsing and recording, I kept Gary close to hand because it's reassuring to look over your shoulder and see, to your mind, one of the best drummers in the world. His playing was a constant feature of both bands: I'd hear the rattle of his snare drum and I would be ready to go. That's definitely how it was when we debuted as a band at a club in Paris. Going abroad to play was a deliberate ploy: we wanted to get away from London and the British media, but, as it turned out, we didn't go quite far enough. The UK music press was out in force, and pretty excited it seemed, and then there were the French on top of that, all their magazines and media, and suddenly it was a bit of a circus – albeit a fun one. If you punch below your weight in terms of venue size, you're going to get excited and disappointed punters outside; it's part of the thrill, part of creating a buzz. It made me feel very welcome, and I realized how much I'd missed it.

Three quick shows in Italy followed, which set the template for Dirty Pretty Things: riotous gigs, unparalleled hedonism and the band finally being marched off a plane at gunpoint and banned from Rimini airport. It had been a strange couple of days anyway. We were trying to pin down our set and find our live sound, and were out with a band with whom I really didn't get on at all. One of them was a real Pete wannabe without any of the songwriting talent, all talk and swagger, who went at the coke and crack with a joyless vengeance, as if it was a part he felt he had to play. He made endless snide digs at the plight of The Libertines, suggesting we, Dirty Pretty Things, were no more than its runt offspring, which was obviously something I didn't need – then or at any time. It was horrific and pathetic and it made me so fucking angry. I was in such a wounded place anyway and I began to hate him; I wasn't sure I could stop myself from laying into him, so I decided the best course of action was to avoid him and his band at all costs.

Odious support acts aside, I was pretty pleased with our progress. There was a lot of positive energy surrounding us, the shows had been warmly received and I felt we had a foundation we could build on. We were in a celebratory mood when we got to the airport, a mood that received a boost when they bumped us up to first class. That was, it's fair to say, a mistake. We were a total fucking mess, rabid and pissed as we took our seats on the plane, a real stupid cliché. And then I felt a hand on my shoulder. I looked around: first, a very camp trolley dolly with an overblown attitude, who was deftly rebuffed; second, a policeman, his hand on his revolver. A policeman, moreover, for each band member, and they didn't look like they were joking either. So they marched us off, removed our clobber from the hold and told us that we were no longer welcome, and that we should go to a different airport if we wanted to get home. From first class to being dragged to the exit and told not to return: it was a sudden fall from grace. I'm not sure if the ban still stands – I haven't been back to find out.

The tour manager took us back to the hotel, where we refused to go to bed: we had loads of gear and we wanted to polish it off before we got on the next plane. On a later tour we'd spend something like £14,000 on cocaine, yet still I didn't think we were out of control. Or maybe I did and I just didn't care. Coke seemed essential then: it gave everything its colour and stopped sleep from being a necessity, and we just wouldn't throw any away. It was a recurring problem for a lot of bands I've known and played with. All too often you ended up forcing yourself to ingest it because you knew you had a customs check coming up.

Even though I'd enjoyed the first four Dirty Pretty Things shows so far, I was as petrified of going on stage as I ever was when I had Peter at my side, maybe more so, as I still didn't really know if I was going to get bottles chucked at me for not being with Peter. The passion we'd inspired together was amazing, and I was pleased people cared so deeply and vocally about us, but after our separation I feared that the violent passions would turn negative – and my reaction to those fears was not good. I thought about Peter a lot, and guessed that he might have been receiving the same treatment, although I think he'd probably deny it. I was still carrying the pain and the shame for the disintegration of my first band – in truth, I'm still devastated about it – whereas at that time I should have just said: 'This is what I am doing, and these are my reasons.'

People sometimes ask me what Dirty Pretty Things gave me

that The Libertines didn't. I stop and think about, and I come to the conclusion that the answer's two-pronged: I got a certain ease and a sense of self-worth. I'd see that ease in other bands and I'd think: *They don't have that bullshit that me and Peter had, they're mates.* Now I realize that I never really saw beneath the veneer, but for a while that's what I thought I wanted. And that sense of relaxation that I'd always striven for in the past actually left me a lot less prolific, because I didn't have another person to push me in that unique way. The sense of worth from Dirty Pretty Things came from not being judged in Peter's shadow, something that I always wanted and eventually came to be. Judging by the crowds at our shows, there were two sorts of fans. The morbid car-crash enthusiasts, attracted by the whole tabloid media thing around Peter, accounted for a fair few bums on seats. But there were also the real fans, to whom I feel so grateful. I was actually pleasantly surprised how well I did on my own; I avoided my own downbeat prognostications.

* * *

Touring with Dirty Pretty Things felt good. It felt like we were doing things for the first time. There's a little bit of footage on my video camera from one of our tours: we're being driven in the bus, and we're just hitting Dover on our way to adventures on the Continent. We'd been up all night and the sun was coming up and we were in the back lounge of the bus with our guitars, and 'Best Days' by Blur is playing on the stereo, and it's just so picture-perfect. If you saw it in a film you'd think it was just a heavy-handed, symbol-laden image, especially as it was my birthday. But when it happens in real life, moments like that are simply beautiful. There's a true togetherness, a oneness. You know the moments like that are what certainly kept it alive.

I look back at those patches of calm, and I know this sounds odd but I think of the film *Stand By Me*. Four kids together on a journey, a certain innocence . . . and I say that fully aware of the body at the end of the road. The niggling insecurity that ambition puts deep in your belly, which I'd learnt about in The Libertines, unquenchable, like the mild depression that I suffer. I found it difficult ever to feel completely happy, and that the moment wasn't somehow overshadowed by future events. Only on stage, experiencing that overflow of strong emotions, was that insecurity quelled and was I truly in the moment. Only that fizz of euphoria could momentarily block out the bad thoughts and fill the void.

I'm getting away from myself again.

I wanted to talk about the way the light hits the buildings in Mexico City, and how I got my driving licence without once taking a lesson. The TV show *Fifth Gear* once asked me to appear, but I doubt their researchers had done their work: I can't drive. We were in Mexico to play some shows and our management, as ever, were trying to do three things at once: shows, a live video and a promo for 'Bang Bang You're Dead', too. We were hanging around in Mexico City, with Mario Galvan – our key to the city, our communicator and, when it came to it, our muscle – a tremendously dependable, kind-hearted being with a strange predilection for *South Park* and blowing things up. Later on, in London, he was to become my flatmate. Mario took me down to a government office, their DVLA equivalent I suppose (though I doubt you'd get away with it in Wales), and fixed it, with the aid of a man who knew a man, that for around four hundred American dollars I was issued with a driving licence. You can see me in the video driving a vintage Mustang we'd hired for the shoot, though it dawned on me fairly quickly that I might start killing children and innocents if I were behind a wheel too long, especially given my drug intake at the time. I only actually drove in about two shots, but I kept the licence until a subsequent girlfriend threw it off a ferry from Dover to Calais. She said she was angry, and I do believe she was. I remember the licence clearing the handrail and disappearing into the choppy waters of the English Channel as if it were yesterday. I don't have any recollection of what she was angry about, though.

We did two gigs in Mexico City, both quite unconventional. One was in the middle of something resembling a council estate, four blocks, in a square and in the middle an empty lot where there had once been a similar building, a space that had been commandeered as an artistic haven. It had large ditches around it, like a moat, filled with burnt-out cars painted orange and yellow and red – like flames, now that I think about it. Atmospheric: a great place to do a show. Or so we thought. We started sound-checking around two in the afternoon, and all the balconies quickly filled with very angry locals staring at us and putting their hands over their ears. We ignored them at first, but then three hours before gig time the Mayor of Mexico City's son rolled up – it turned out he lived around the corner – and said we could only proceed if we gave him some sort of donation. I'm not sure what we were donating to, but it cost us a few grand to go on with that show. Given the whole driving licence situation, I shouldn't really have been so surprised when that happened.

You can actually see some of that show in the video for 'Bang Bang You're Dead', and we followed that up by playing a disused bank, which had real bullet holes in the ceiling, from what I liked to imagine were banditos. That place must have been at least three hundred years old, and when we stepped out on to the stage the audience was full of kids who'd travelled something like ten hours to see us, really Amazonian looking; it all felt so exotic. I really did have a moment where I couldn't believe the power of music, how far it could reach; people were so happy that we'd made the effort to come. There's not much money in playing in those sorts of places, so most bands don't bother doing it. They should, though: it was like experiencing Beatlemania.

There were more drugs in Mexico City than even we might have imagined, incredible cocaine called Coconut Grove, presumably after the area or the song. The way it was explained to me made no sense, but I'll share it anyway as I was fascinated. Coconut Grove was a kilo of cocaine that was dissolved in coconut milk and then dried and distilled, and then condensed down to only 600 grams of lethal cocaine-coconut mixture. I should have asked for the recipe, because the result meant that snorting it was like smelling coconut, desiccated coconut; it was really rather lovely. There'd just be a lovely rush accompanied by a coconut scent that made you feel as if you were luxuriating in a very expensive spa. It really was quite special. When people ask me now if they can get it, I say, of course you can: just go to Mexico City.

I stayed in Mexico for a few weeks with Mario Galvan; it was fair to say that he knew how things worked. We shot some of the 'Bang Bang' video around the old streets where Frida Kahlo's house is, playing the trumpet and moving through the city, riding in cars balanced on flatbed trailers. It was like a film set, and tremendous fun, with people wandering around with walkie-talkies, a crew and security guards – lots of security guards. Not that we ever needed them – or not that we noticed. That's the thing about good security: if it's done well then it's a deterrent and you don't need to use them.

I was glad they were around, though, later. We were on the way to see the Aztec pyramids, which, again, we were planning to shoot for use in the video. I'd never seen death before. I've seen it in films and on the TV, I've seen graphic violence on the street at kicking-out time, but watching someone meet a bloody, violent end is not something you generally wake up thinking about: you don't expect to have to look into the maw before the afternoon's over. On the way to the pyramids we had to pass through an old, dangerous *barrio* where there was a lot of gang trouble – where, apparently, when they'd been shooting the film *Man on Fire*, a gang of machine-gun toting guys had calmly demanded two of the Ford people-carriers the production was using. And the film people, of course, just gave them right over. What else could they do?

That's the kind of neighbourhood we were in when Roger Sargent, our photographer, decided we needed to get out for some pictures. Roger was an old friend, who'd come to one of our earliest gigs at the Albion Rooms in Bethnal Green. He has a roaringly infectious laugh and a strange and unbridled passion for the Second World War, which is reinforced by his occasional resemblance to a young Churchill. He's taken some of the most iconic music photos of a generation, so we followed him out of the car, but immediately it felt bad, that kind of bad that makes your guts itch, and I looked around and realized that even our security guys were bricking it. They knew better than us just how lawless it was down there. We were trying to look casual as we strolled down these little streets and alleyways, then Roger suddenly started shouting at us, and other people in our group started shouting too, and we quickly jumped back in the car, hearts beating out of our chest, mouths dry, and as we're tearing out of there, there's a young man getting lynched. He had what looked like barbed wire round his neck, surrounded by a big gang who were kicking and punching him, and dragging him along the street, off to his death. I'd say it was horrific, but that doesn't begin to describe it. Even now, writing this, I can still see his body kicking up dust, his feet flailing uselessly as he's pulled off towards his doom. Someone took a photo on their camera; someone else muttered about local justice, but I didn't know how to react. All I remember is in that hot Mexican sun everything suddenly turned cold, bleached of its colour like old bones.

SEVEN

Truth Begins

In hindsight, perhaps I should have packed it in when the record company called me up as I was getting ready to record our second album and said, 'Just write another twelve songs like "Bang Bang You're Dead" and you'll be fine.' Then again, perhaps it should have been when Didz and I stumbled on to the set of *Soccer AM* clutching our pints of milk, weaving towards an alarmed looking Helen Chamberlain and Tim Lovejoy. We'd played Wolverhampton the night before, and I was quite ill – it seems as if I'm always ill – so we'd got some extra gear in to compensate, to keep me going. I remember going into makeup early that bright morning and rolling about a bit and the people in there exchanging startled glances. We hadn't slept and all we wanted was a drink; both of these things might have been obvious to anyone tuning in to the show as they munched their cornflakes and sipped their coffee or Alka-Seltzer. We were pursuing a rather more radical path of hangover abatement, that of pushing on through and drinking into the middle of the following week, but unsurprisingly, if disappointingly, the green room at the Sky studios in west London didn't have a wet bar, or if it did then it wasn't stocked at nine in the morning. Which was why we opted for milk: it came in pints and the heft of it felt good in the hand. I think when Didz spat milk all over Tim Lovejoy's shirt that Tim was less enamoured of our idea. He wasn't that keen on us in general, I suspect, but, to his credit, he didn't force the bottle up Didz's nose, only made an aside about how bad it would smell later and soldiered on. If I could have focused on him, I would almost certainly have been impressed. For respite, they cut to a montage of the season's best goals so far, and Didz leant over to the equally impassive Helen Chamberlain as she was reading the voiceover accompanying the goals being neatly slotted in on the monitor. 'When,' asked the listing Didz, 'does this go out on TV?' His question was audible to everyone in the studio and at home. Didz has one of the most advanced senses of humour I've ever come across and, for better or worse, his sarcasms sometimes cancel each other out, so that it can seem like there wasn't a joke to begin with. Helen gave him a look like he'd just kicked her grandmother.

'It's live.'

After we came back from the commercial break they'd wisely moved us down the sofa, where I found myself next to a grinning Noel Gallagher, who was politeness and charm personified as I attempted to chew my own face off. I watched our performance again on YouTube the other night, and I look almost innocent in my admiration of the older Gallagher; innocent if you don't count the half-pound of chang stuck up my nose. You can watch it yourself: the presenters ask me a question that bounces off like a child's rubber-tipped arrow, and I turn to Noel, possibly a little bit in love, forgetting about the cameras, the dumbfounded studio guests and production crew. I haven't slept for a few days and our gig in Wolverhampton the night before is a distant memory, but it is a new dawn, I feel alive and I have something important to say. It is vital stuff, I am sure. 'That song,' I stutter, and launch into a good three minutes of garbled, nonsensical drivel. There is an Oasis song I really, really love and it is crucial that Noel and the viewing audience know its life-shattering, life-affirming significance, but try as I might I can't remember what it is called. I go around and around like a man adrift in a dinghy with only one paddle searching for the lever in my memory that would set its title free. Noel lays a reassuring hand on my arm. I am rapt. 'Live Forever', he says, to which I react as if he's dropped a bottle of Scotch in my lap. I am delighted.

Soccer AM told us we couldn't come back after that. We had two producers and a floor manager shouting at us: they made it pretty clear that we weren't welcome. So we departed, out of the doors into the bright sun and as quickly as we could to the nearest off-licence, to get back on the horse, so to speak. We were doing a BBC Radio One gig that night and I'm certain we didn't sleep before that either: we got a day room in a hotel and just kept going, cresting waves of totally lucidity before falling apart once again. Strangely, word of mouth spread about our appearance, and the viewing figures for our segment shot through the roof; so I think they did call us up again. The next time we slept beforehand . . . at least I think we did.

* * *

Dirty Pretty Things reconvened on the US West Coast for album number two, with Nick Leman as our producer. We'd been introduced by Alan McGee, our mentor, friend and manager, the trilby-wearing Glaswegian who'd discovered Oasis and who took The Libertines on during their darkest hour and guided them through tempestuous waters, and I felt a bond with Nick. He was a former commando, though not so much in his manner. He was laid back and charming and I really took to him: he was an intelligent and enigmatic man and we got on well on many levels. But, and I don't mean to slight him in any way, he also had a darkness, a thousand-yard stare, and a great sadness somewhere beneath the surface – and this assessment from a man who can be about as cheery as a wet winter's morning. Leman was working making advertising jingles, a very lucrative gig as far as I could tell, at a place called Amber Music, which was on Stewart Boulevard in Los Angeles, but right at the arse end, between the Marina and Santa Monica. It was just a wasteland really, though we were in the same building as Larry David; all the exterior shots of the office in *Curb Your Enthusiasm* were done there. The oddest thing about the studio was that it was housed in an office block, so in the daytime it was bubbling, filled with people creating jingles and a real office vibe: people you didn't know would wave at you and hope you'd have a nice day. Consequently it was vaguely sterile and really not at all conducive to making music. We were based in the complex's central unit, a huge room with a plush pool table and a big TV, with all the little studios radiating off it like satellite moons off a planet, but with much, much less charm. We might as well have been in Slough for all the feelings of California it evoked.

Nevertheless, the location was bearable and Nick was fine. The real trouble came in the shape of Miguel, a Chicano drug dealer who would do you an eight ball for a hundred bucks and, like the best pizza places, deliver it for free. We called him round every evening. There was a kitchen area where, mainly at night, we spent a lot of time drinking wine and losing the will to live, Miguel coming in and out of the shadows. After a while, cabin fever broke out, madness ensued and rows started happening that just shouldn't have. Punctuality, which had once existed, went straight out of the window and we started focusing on ridiculous things, getting totally het up over nothing: *if we use this drum sound on this track it's going to make the album it'll be great it'll be perfect if we don't use this keyboard on this track it's going to ruin the record.* Endless chatter, inane, drug-fuelled crap at a million miles an hour, and Gary standing in the corner, not touching the stuff, but having to listen to all this bloody drivel.

We'd hired a little apartment about three boring miles from the studio, opposite a strip mall and miles from anywhere, which only fuelled the madness as we had nowhere to go and nothing to do. The boredom hurt us and we were wearing on each other. My philosophy as far as that band went was a democratic one: we should all have an equal say in things, but, we were finding out, that probably doesn't work in a band no matter how hard you try. In social terms, it was like taking a group of romance novelists and asking them to have an informed view on quantum physics or space travel. That's a mangled analogy at best, but trust me when I say that not everyone in a band can be equal. I blame myself. I wanted the togetherness of a gang so much that I was blind to the practicalities of what I was doing. I was a lost boy and I needed that feeling, and I didn't feel I was part of that brotherhood by being boss. I wanted that whole die-for-each other vibe, which I'd had with Peter. I just wanted it back, I guess.

Within two weeks everything had gone pretty pear-shaped and we'd got precious little done – guide tracks to three tunes at best. The plan had been that a lot of the songs were to be written in the studio, and we had worked up fragments and ideas, but nothing was coming out and none of us were getting on. We were pretending to be a gang, but I think we were all unsure about our roles and who was running the show, or where the material was meant to be coming from. Everyone was vying for their stuff to be used, and there was no clear main writer. Things were moving very slowly, and it was getting tougher every day. What we didn't realize was that Miguel was cutting the coke with crystal meth. A month later and things were totally out of hand.

We knew pretty early on it wasn't working. Ask us why it wasn't working, however, and we couldn't have told you. We were completely blind, just oblivious, and yet coming up with meth-fuelled, crazy-radical suggestions. At one point we decided to move back to England and finish it, and it became an ongoing squabble, but nothing ever happened. We'd troop across the road at the end of each session, thoroughly deflated and wired, to these apartments that might as well have been on a Basingstoke trading estate, and just flop down and wonder what the hell we were going to do. I feel sorry for the guy from the label who'd been sent out there to mediate; he had quite a job on his hands, and he can't have been aware of 90 per cent of what was really going on.

We finally came home three months after we'd left, feeling shabby from the whole experience, only to discover the entire fucking album was recorded on 8-bit instead of 16-bit, which meant the master wasn't even up to the sound quality of a bog-standard CD. Not only that, but it was littered with various weird little oversights and errors, which meant we had to make all sorts of different mixes and loads of overdubs. It was a complete and utter ball-ache. The label had budgeted £25,000, and I dread to think how far we went over, only to come back with an album that wasn't even properly recorded.

For all its flaws, though, there are some beautiful songs on there. Some of the details are exquisite. There's a song called 'Truth Begins' that I like very much, that means a lot to me. That's probably my personal high point of the album. But it's a record that's hard to go back to; it's like photos of the one that got away. I've not really been able to look at it since. Actually, there are some wonderful moments on that record, but I might need to give it another year before I play it again . . .

The record company really wanted 'Tired Of England' as the first single, which was a song that caused us absolute murder, a perfect example, in fact, of how democracy signals the end of a great song. It happened so many times on the album: we'd start writing a song and nail the beginning. But where to go next? I'd canvass everyone's opinion, and a few ideas would result. Maybe a couple would be promising, but because I was too mindful of getting a consensus, we'd never pursue anything to its end, to the point where everything superfluous had been pared away, and only the essentials remained. Nobody took responsibility, and because I wasn't forceful enough at pushing everyone to make something as good as it could be, too afraid of hurting feelings or bruising egos, I let it lie. Nothing outstanding is ever created without a strong vision, and I knew that 'Tired Of England' was good, but in my heart of hearts I knew it could have been better. Yet for the sake of democracy I said, 'Okay, that's that then, that's finished. Song done.'

The bad decisions were also due, in part, to my laziness. It's happened at many times in my life: people around me have said, 'It's fine', and I've just wanted an easy life, an easy way out, and so I've agreed. Combine the 'democracy' with fear and the laziness, and I'd usually just say, 'Okay, let's go with that.' Invariably, this has been the wrong decision. In this particular case, the decisions came back to haunt me when the label plucked it out of the air and announced it was going to be the first single. 'Tired Of England' is still to my mind an unfinished song, and it festers guiltily at the back of my brain.

* * *

Romance At Short Notice was slightly unloved, and we didn't tour it that hard. An album not being much of a commercial success hadn't happened to me before, but we made it work live, as we always did. We did give it a shot, took it on a journey, and it took us to some strange places, too. The five-star hotel in Moscow felt to me as if it had been built on the bones of the poor, fuelled by drug money and the blood of innocents – I was half expecting a professional hit in the opulent surroundings of the bar. It was one of the most incredible places we'd ever seen as a band, gothic and austere with brooding marble monsters mounted at the top of the stairs and busts along the hallways, but it was combined with a ridiculous level of service, plush furnishings, huge beds and grand windows with the kind of views the tsars must have enjoyed before the axe fell. From the roof terrace you could marvel at Red Square, the imperial past set free by revolutionaries, laid out down below. I found a little button next to the bed that caused a Perspex tablet to slide out, like something out of *Star Trek*. On its surface there were little icons, some of which – drinks and room service – were obvious; one of them, however, a picture of a woman, seemed to hold the promise of mystery. Given the decadence and licentiousness of the surroundings, we thought, *Wow, that must be prostitutes.* What happens if we push that one?

We didn't ponder on that too long, but took off into the Russian night at a clip. We went and got spangled on a Moscow adventure, hopping in and out of dodgy illegal cabs, narrowly avoiding getting bummed and drugged, finding amazing little drinking taverns, as you'd imagine in Berlin at its most decadent, sleazy cabaret bars that were just perfect for the way we were feeling. When we returned, the room felt like a palace, and we began goading each other on. It was five in the morning and we were absolutely hammered – and for once we weren't blitzed on coke; it was all good old-fashioned Russian vodka, the kind that tears your innards apart. Like Pandora and her box, Eve and her apple, we couldn't resist temptation – temptation was the one thing we could never resist – so we pushed the button, the icon of the lady, and waited nervously, laughing, for the best part of an hour. Just as we were getting annoyed at its apparent non-function, and running out of steam, there was a knock on the door. We snap to attention and tidy ourselves up and arrange our hair, then gingerly open the door while trying to reassure each other, *Oh, it's just going to be a massage*, and standing there is a very confused looking cleaner. And us, a couple of goons with sloppy smiles, staring back.

Looking back, it's no wonder that I came home from that trip and got fucking pancreatitis. I wonder now if we all knew that the band was coming to an end, and so tried to make every night like it was our last on earth.

* * *

The turning point came, though, when we were in Brighton, due to play the Concorde II. I wasn't happy, and was self-medicating again, blanking from consciousness whole swathes of my diary, and the unavoidable conclusion was that the band was the reason why. I kept trying to make something work that just wouldn't, like going back to the wrong girl over and over again. I had to stop. I knew I didn't have the confidence to go it alone, so I didn't know what was going to happen after, but I knew I couldn't go on. That was the important thing.

I was walking along the front and down towards the pier, seagulls milling in the warm air against that golden light you sometimes get by the water. I could smell chips and doughnuts, salty and sweet in interchangeable gusts of sea air. Anthony was with me, fumbling for change in his pocket as we walked into the arcade, a domed roof filled with ringing bells and synthesized voices coming from the machines. I sat down and told him my decision, which was quite a big thing as I'd not told the others yet, told him first because he was my closest friend in the band and it felt like he'd been with me for the long haul. And then, as we're walking up the pier, out of nowhere a couple of girls came running up, shouting and screaming, 'Oh my God, oh Carl, you completely changed our lives.'

There was an enthusiastic innocence to them; they were so thrilled that I happened to be there. They both showed me the 'libertine' tattoo on their ankles, very much like the one Peter and I share. I asked them if they were coming to the show that night, and they genuinely had no clue that we were playing. I think I might have invited them, but their faces had changed and they both sort of shrugged; they weren't bothered. A part of me was gutted, but at the same time a part of me thought, *Well, they had their moment with you, and they cherish that. They hold that dear. They didn't need to be those girls forever, they moved on. You were their soundtrack for a while, so much so that they tattooed you on to their skin, and that's okay, that's all right.* Actually, that's beautiful and I'm proud to have been part of it. Don't get me wrong: if I'd seen that last scene played out in a cinema, I would have been throwing popcorn at the screen, but it was a very poignant moment and it's really stayed with me.

I couldn't walk out of Dirty Pretty Things there and then, we had too many commitments, but it was certainly the beginning of the end. I remember the band being scared but they were all quite noble about it. I felt worst for Didz because he had three kids to look after. I felt like their fate weighed on me, but I had to come to terms with the fact that everyone else's incomes weren't my responsibility. I also felt like I'd sold myself short, by shirking the mantle of leadership, by pretending not to be the kingpin and trying to avoid confrontation, trying to be diplomatic all the time.

* * *

Overall, I'm glad the band's over now, and that we all left essentially on good terms – such a nice change compared to the last band. Some Japanese kids in London were recently asking me if we were ever going to play again, and I bumped into some kids in LA who asked me about Dirty Pretty Things as well. That was a breath of fresh air after spending years of my life listening to people asking about The Libertines. It's nice to realize that a lot of kids were into them without being into The Libertines first. We had one and a half good records, like The Strokes at that time, and they did all right.

I learnt a lot through Dirty Pretty Things, learnt a lot the hard way. They taught me to go solo, that I had to stand on my own two feet, go it alone. If I've lamented Dirty Pretty Things here in these pages, then that's easy to do when it's late at night and red wine has taken a hold. It's easy to get maudlin as you pore over old pictures and look at journal entries, and wonder where that person went. But Dirty Pretty Things was the adventure I needed when The Libertines went south. We played every show like it was our last. I guess you always should, but that feeling can get lost far too quickly and easily. There was always a great energy and a lot of spirit; we were, for want of a better term, always really on it. Even after we knew it was ending we managed to retain that. I'm proud of us all for doing so.

EIGHT

A Bird in the Hand

When I came to, she was standing over me in knickers and a white vest, Swedish as I remember it, and I had a brief mental playback of the night before. There'd been a Libertines show at the famous Hope and Anchor pub on Upper Street; it was early in the band's life and, to celebrate my progress in overcoming my creeping stage fright, I'd gone on to have a real night of it, and had been approached by a girl after the show as I stood by the bar. Lying there, I began to think how playing in a band was all right by me, but my reverie was shattered when I realized my special new friend had no idea who her bed companion was. First there was noise, which mainly consisted of her screaming 'Get out!' at ever-increasing volume. Her face, so pretty the night before, was now lined and angry. She started kicking me, and then a punch went into my ribs, making me gasp and realize how hungover I was. This is broadening my spectrum of experience considerably, I thought, as she let off a canister of CS spray in my face. Now, you may know all about this, may be one of those people who likes to attend marches and goad police dogs, but if you've never had CS gas in your face I really don't recommend it, and especially when you're in nothing but your pants. I tried to remonstrate with her, foolishly as it turned out, as opening my mouth meant that I actually swallowed some of the stuff. She kicked me in the shins as I hopped around on one foot, one leg stuck in my jeans like I was Brian Rix in a West End farce. I half ran, half stumbled out of the door, and stood in the street wheezing and rubbing at my eyes with my T-shirt. I'd been wearing our bass player's hat the night before, and I realized I'd left it behind. He'd be less than pleased with me, but there was no way I was going back. I hacked my lungs out some more, straightened up and asked a quizzical looking passer-by where the Tube might be.

* * *

I'll lay my cards on the table – the kitchen table, to be precise. I've been no saint. It's late and my girlfriend's upstairs, asleep. She's tired because she's carrying our baby, and I'm sitting here with the kitchen door open, smoking a cigarette that I shouldn't be, hoping the night air will carry the smoke and the smell away. It might sound mawkish, but it wouldn't be exaggerating to say that she saved me from myself. When I think back now to the places I've been, the things I've seen and done, I feel ashamed, but I shan't turn away from the man I once was.

Blisters on my skin aside, that night was a bit of a lesson, an eye-opener about the whole being-on-stage thing. You standing up there on a bit of wood just a foot or two higher than everyone else somehow acts as a ridiculous aphrodisiac for some women – a fact that, at the time, seemed like a burgeoning recompense for enduring stage fright. The notion of someone wanting to have sex with you because you're carrying a guitar is gross, but still you end up doing it because you have certain flesh-and-blood needs and, besides, you're only human. I was weak: I became as addicted to smut as I did to cocaine and Jameson's Special Reserve. It became part of the game, back when my life was a game and not like real life at all.

* * *

I think it was a 'rock star' – let's say it was someone from Kiss – who said don't fall in love with the girls you meet on tour, because when you leave there's always another bus coming through town. I've known plenty of girls who have wanted to be with the band, and their motives are still a mystery to me. When we first went to Scotland as The Libertines, two sisters turned up after a gig, just oozing sex and dark possibilities, and instantly offered me a threesome in the toilet. I don't think it was the first time they'd been in that scenario, and the thing that struck me was just how pretty they were, and how desperate to do the filthiest things, all at the tender age of seventeen or thereabouts. It wasn't salacious, it was grim, though if I'm honest a lot of the reason why I didn't disappear into a cubicle with them was fear. I was intimidated by the whole business and sort of had to teach myself to be filthier, to lose my inhibitions.

I've said it elsewhere, but I was a late bloomer in many ways, and especially when it came to girls. As a shy teenager in Whitchurch, my friends – what friends I had – were leaving me far behind. At the very least, they certainly talked like they were. At the start of my teenage years, I thought girls were a different species, inhabiting a different world, but love eventually came and got me at fifteen. My first real girlfriend was a little younger than me, and we were together for nine months, which is an eternity when you're a teenager. We did all that nauseating stuff on the phone, the 'I love you, no, no . . . you hang up first . . ', a terrible cliché in many bad films, but actually, and embarrassingly, true. I'd fumbled my way around other girls before then: there'd been plenty of extremely uncomfortable moments trying to undo bodysuits on park benches in the dark, followed, once the breakthrough had been made, by not really knowing what to do once you got there – the definition, perhaps, of a hollow victory. Those bodysuits were a Gordian knot, far better than a medieval chastity belt at deterring the average teenage boy. They really were hard work. You'd be slaving away, driven like Dr Sam Beckett by some unknown force, and the bodysuit would render the whole affair utterly unsexy. Bringing them to mind conjures up apologetic memories, clumsy thumbs and stuck clasps, wilting passion. Awkward, gauche conversations:

'Shall we do this . . . Do you mind if I . . .?'

'Yes, you may now touch my breast.'

So very, very unsexy.

It was frustrating because my friends were obviously more driven than I was by their urges and instincts – to the point of not giving a fuck – and their attitude, perversely in my eyes, seemed to win them greater popularity with girls.

France, too, had a role to play in my sentimental education, in the form of a girl called Solène, who also inspired a song, the rather imaginatively titled 'France'. I was eighteen, living in Stockwell, and she came from a small town outside Paris and couldn't have seemed more exotic. She was the first truly beautiful girl I'd ever dated. I think the fact that she was French helped, though that worked against us eventually. She'd returned home in floods of tears with the promise that I'd go and visit her one day, but when that day came for me to board the bus to France I couldn't do it. I couldn't connect with her culturally, and I couldn't cope with the idea of it all. Worst of all, I failed to tell her before the bus arrived in Paris, so she was there to meet me, watching the bus empty and I wasn't on it. I put her through the mill, something I'm still sorry about now. I wrote her that song, but she never spoke to me again. I've no idea if she even liked it.

*   *   *

At first, when touring with the band, I was still green, and I'd often mistake the intense attention we received from our fans for ardour, which led to some awkward situations. I'd make the move, that fatal lunge, and instead of willingly acquiescing, they'd be devastated. It's a sticky, silent moment: all she wants to do is read you her poetry, or show you the painting she's done of the band, and you've made it clear that you want something completely different – you're nothing but an insensitive misogynist and the embodiment of all the worst clichés about musicians. In truth, all I ever wanted was a little love, which is the kind of thinking that can get you into all sorts of strange trouble. I used to try and keep the girls going for more than one night, as if we were in the first bloom of love, that each time, each coupling, was something with the potential to last. I was fooling myself, though I'm not sure I was fooling them. Naïvety, drink, drugs or simple bad judgement? It was one, or a combination, of those that sustained that delusion. I have to romanticize everything, even girls whose idea of a good time is being filmed by a drummer while she gyrates on a tour bus.

One of the saddest things about the groupie life, I discovered, was the brazen ambition of it all. Girls would start off aiming at the highest point, the singer or guitarist, say, and then, if they failed, move on down the pecking order, until they ended up sleeping with the big fat guitar tech. Everyone had a sort of value and a place in the hierarchy, and there were plenty of guys working in the crew who knew their place, but were content to wait to catch the scraps from the lion's table, like vultures. Band members' mates, people hanging around backstage, even journalists got lucky. I'd see naïve young women just starting out, but already committed to that lifestyle, and I'd think, *Don't do this.* I'd even try to talk to them sometimes, but they'd just think I was patronizing them. And I knew full well that the day our bus pulled out, the next one would roll into town; you couldn't ever really save them.

I confess, however, that my moral compass wasn't always pointing in the right direction, and often I'd delight in the random, impersonal physical encounters. I remember moments, the backs of buses, grabbing hands in toilet stalls, walking through the audience, slippery and pliant, and any number of hands, female hands, just all over me and thinking, *Why are these hands on me? I'm disgusting and wet.* They'd go for my chest and back and occasionally my arm and, if I was high on MDMA, I used to think it was incredibly sexy. Different countries would offer up different kinds of decorum. If you kissed a girl in a Scandinavian country, it seemed the sex would be a foregone conclusion, that within seconds she'd have taken all her clothes off and be assisting you as best she could in separating you from yours. It could get very frenzied; it must have been something to do with the cold weather. And, although I was learning to play the game, on my way to becoming something of a rogue, there were times when I'd miss all the signs. I'd watch guys in my band kissing the girls and have no idea that that was the green light. I'd sit and watch them, and still try to woo the girl I was with.

The tour bus had a weird protocol, and you quickly learnt where to draw the line – unless, that is, you were one of our crew who we'd come to call Peeping Tim, for obvious reasons. He'd always be in your peripheral vision, staring, but in the rush of the moment and in the desire to acquit yourself favourably, you couldn't really stop and tell him to fuck off. That said, there was definitely an etiquette about how things went in general. For instance, if a girl had been on the bus a while – it was the third day running, say – you had to be careful how you approached things. You had to let her know that it was time to leave the party, go to the nearest station and catch the train of shame; how best to slip the question 'Are you going to get off in Frankfurt?' into the conversation? On the other hand, although there was no point pretending it could go any further, you couldn't just spurn someone who'd maybe crossed borders to spend time with you, with whom you'd spent a few stolen moments of happiness in between performing and unconsciousness. Even when it did all end happily, you often had to give them some money to help them get home, and then it looked and felt like a transaction. And the tour bus, even at the best of times, without the band tensions that spiralled out of control, was a claustrophobic place. Many a grotty morning I'd wake, with a truly thundering hangover and a head filled with cotton wool and cocaine, squashed into my bunk next to someone I didn't know, someone who, two weeks and ten more gigs down the line, I wouldn't have been able to pick out of a police line-up. I'd be vulnerable and paranoid, coming down and with a hint of panic creeping up on me, and I'd struggle out of the bunk to find our rotund tour manager in his pants looking for something on one side of me, and our very fleshy guitar tech on the other, and I'd be trapped between them, enclosed on all sides by flesh, drowning in a sea of pink.

Often you'd get bizarre requests, or get placed in an impossible position. Regularly, after The Libertines finished a show, boys would approach to ask us to kiss their girlfriends. It happened a lot: it was a genuine trend, and one that, frankly, confused the hell out of me. You didn't want to offend a big bloke by not kissing his girlfriend, but then you didn't want to offend him either by kissing his girlfriend and looking like you were enjoying it too much, or, God forbid, if his girlfriend suddenly got into it and tried to latch on. It became really awkward, occasionally, when you'd see an angry, red-faced man standing in the corner looking at the floor, and a girl sauntering towards you. 'My boyfriend and I,' she'd say, with a dismissively pointing finger, 'each have one free pass – one person that we can sleep with, no guilt or shame.' Then the killer punch line: 'Mine is you.'

Riiiiiight.

'You've both got one, have you?' would be my opening gambit, making light of it, and I'd try to hold it at a conversation, though I'd be frantically scanning the room for the nearest exit, plotting an escape, mentally sawing a hole around myself, like Elmer Fudd or Wile E. Coyote, so that I could drop through the floor and disappear. I can still see those guys standing there, their hearts breaking, their girlfriends oblivious.

* * *

Japan provided, in hindsight, one of the most shameful experiences. It was towards the end of The Libertines, I'd met a Japanese girl and, all evening, it had been smiles and giggles, just lovely. So I invited her to join the band for dinner but, later, when it came down to it, she was tense and stiff as a board, not moving a muscle. She would only say 'Hi', which she repeated over and over, and I had to keep asking her if she was all right. Afterwards, I was sort of falling asleep and she began to sob, on the floor in a ball. I panicked, thinking that 'Hi' might be Japanese for 'Stop' and that I'd done something terrible. I had images of me being carted away by the Japanese police, flashbulbs going off, my face all over the British tabloids. I leant across to touch her on the shoulder, asked her what was wrong and she said, tears streaming down her cheeks: 'I was worried that I wasn't good enough for you.' That made me sad; sad for her and sad also that I had helped the whole sorry situation into existence.

From then on, though, she seemed to appear everywhere we went, acting surprised when she saw us, saying, 'Oh my God, you're here!' It was all very calculated and totally at odds with the vulnerable girl who'd been in my hotel room. But then Anthony, who was playing with us as a replacement for Peter, took a shine to her, and began to woo her. He asked her up to the hotel roof with him, to go and look at the stars – even though, as I've said, you often didn't have to woo girls on tour. This situation was a prime demonstration of that fact. All he really had to do was say 'Can you please go inside and take your clothes off?' and she would have done, but his conduct was sweet and refreshing, a moment of normality amongst the madness. Secretly, I was delighted when she'd suddenly turn up in unexpected places and tell Anthony she couldn't believe he was there, too. The coincidence. Who knows? Then one day she caught him hiding. We'd been walking down the street and he'd spotted her and hidden behind a pillar, without realizing that his presence was betrayed, reflected in the glass of the big windows behind him. She burst into tears, and I felt ashamed about the cruelty of it all.

* * *

Sometimes, though, tour life was just plain fun. Every once in a while someone really sound came along, and you'd both be absolutely in the moment, just enjoying it for its own sake. There was a model, for example. I was on tour with Dirty Pretty Things, it was our second album, we were in a fug, and I think we could all hear the wheels slowly coming off, when I met her in Stockholm. You'd have thought I'd have learnt my lesson with Swedish girls, but rational thinking was beyond me at that time, and I can still clearly remember her coming backstage, then kissing after three drinks in some bar we'd gone on to. After that, she just got on the bus with me, not even a change of clothes, and we left. She had a sense of freedom about her that impressed me and made me envious: I wished sometimes that I could detach myself from all life's expectations and hurts and just exist with that kind of fervour, that kind of liberty. She stayed with me on the bus through six different countries, the cities flying by on a cloud of cocaine and booze. 'Why don't you get me pregnant?' she said. 'Just give me a kid, I'll look after it, I won't ask for anything.' And I was so out of it that I agreed. Fortunately, we'd both forgotten about that idea as soon as the words left our mouths. We finally said goodbye when we got to Germany, where I think I paid for her flight home. Later, she got in touch to say she wanted to come and see me in London but, in all honesty, for me it was over, just part of a high-speed, borderline-insane bender that happened in another country. Thankfully, it didn't go anywhere, and it transpired that she had a boyfriend at home anyway. That had never come up in my bunk. Strange the things you neglect to mention when you're out of your mind on coke.

I realize that I'd turned, by that point, into something of a predator. We'd be pulling up to the venues and there'd be fans already outside. A pretty one would catch my eye, and I'd make a mental note of her face while I rid myself of the previous night's girl, making sure she could get home safely. It's crass and shameful, but for a while it seemed like the most normal thing in the world. My second band was falling apart almost as tragically as the first, and I was watching the world drift by in a hungover haze, desperate for any kind of escape. I had so little self-worth by that stage. Genuinely, a lot of the time, I'd think, or hope, that we'd be embarking on these trysts on an equal footing, that she, whoever she was, just wanted a little fun. Then I'd find that, pressed to give more of myself, I upset a lot of girls when I made it clear that I didn't want to see them after what I believed was the relationship's natural conclusion. The meltdown and recriminations always took me by surprise.

Later, when I went solo, I was crashing out of control while supporting Glasvegas on their US tour, a drunken animal still stuck in the old patterns of behaviour. And Glasvegas were so bloody gracious to me – I'd organize impromptu parties on their bus and they'd be fine with it. At my worst, I stole two girls from James (the band's vocalist and actually a good, and hopefully forgiving, friend) who was in the back of the bus, being gentlemanly and charming and slowly working his magic. I, on the other hand, stumbled cross-eyed and ruined into the party, leapt on one, grabbed the other, and left. Glasvegas were going to Canada the next day, and I couldn't follow as I wouldn't have been able to re-enter the States, so I took them off to my Seattle hotel, leaving James, dejected, on the bus on his own. In Glasvegas's position, I'd have given me a swift kick up the arse and left me at an all-night gas station to fend for myself. The mess was compounded by the fact that I'd already kissed a different girl that same night, who was something to do with Glasvegas's record company; she'd tried to come on the bus with me, but Glasvegas hadn't wanted her to. There'd been a stand-off, and, when she'd grabbed my arm, pleaded with me to stay with her, I ran away. I always did. I got on the bus.

I've spent so many nights doing that: pushing the eject button, moving on, looking for the next thing, trying to find something better, someone more beautiful, trying to fill the void. I'm aware of how selfish that sounds. I'd spend countless nights looking over people's shoulders, working the room and then everything would blur, and after a while I'd come to and find all the girls I'd been talking to were long gone – each convinced, perhaps, that I was going off with someone else. Perhaps they were simply bored with being played. I'd weave down the hotel corridor in a stupor, get one last drink at the bar, slur my goodnights to the receptionist and flop down on my bed, the lamp hurting my eyes. I'd wonder where I was and then it would hit me: I was on my own. And I'd wait quietly for sleep to come.

* * *

I can only look back at this so much; it's getting late, and I've smoked too many cigarettes. London's quiet now, the house is still, and I realize I've come to the crux of the matter. All I really wanted was company; I never wanted to go to the hotel on my own. I'm not a great fan of my own company and I'm not making excuses for my behaviour, but I did find comfort in some strangers' arms and legs. I'd probably advocate that lifestyle if the backstage sex was just pure sporting fun, if it was ever done without guilt or guile, but that's just not the way it was. And the sad thing is that I always desperately hoped that I'd meet a woman at my shows, someone I really did want to be with, who I genuinely got on with, who shared my taste in books and art; someone who was level-headed, beautiful inside and out. But, even if she had been there, it wasn't as if I could have gone out into the crowds to seek her out – I wouldn't have got ten yards without being mobbed. Unfortunately, that sort of girl, the one I imagined I wanted to meet, rarely tries to push her way backstage. She doesn't want to be mistaken for a groupie. So you drink another shot and end up talking to the girls who are milling around and trying to catch your eye, looking like sharks that have smelt blood in the water – though I realize now I was the shark.

NINE

Songs of Experience

If some of the earlier chapters of this book read like a succession of sense impressions loosely connected by a thin thread of consciousness dipping and diving into oblivion under the influence of various substances, well, that's what my life was like, for years, with both bands. And, once Dirty Pretty Things was over, I had a lot of time to myself, time during which I continued partying, on autopilot, without thinking about what I was doing or where I was going. I liked the recklessness of not sleeping. I'd sleep maybe Monday, Wednesday and Friday, fading in and out, living a white noise existence, having parties at random and hoards of people over, sitting around in front of an unlit fire in the front room waiting for a dealer to come around, until I would suddenly look up and realize I didn't recognize half the people sitting around me. How had they got in? Had I met them in the pub? And who'd invited them back? All of which only served to ratchet up the paranoia on top of all that coke that's making you bug-eyed anyway.

* * *

Growing up, there was very little to do in Whitchurch apart from drink, take drugs and think about sex. My first can of cider – it's always cider first, isn't it? – lasted me for about a week; I'd take a few swigs every night to make me feel different and quietly convince myself that I was now off my face. I was unpopular at school, or, if not actually unpopular, just invisible, until, when I was fourteen, my mother moved and I had access to a neighbour's greenhouse where they were growing dope. I used to steal a bud or two whenever I wanted – after all, it wasn't as if they could report me to the police if they caught me jumping over the wall with a fistful of their weed. So I quickly became the man with the plan, everyone's favourite friend. Weed, though, sent me west, something I worked out pretty quickly, so I knocked it on the head at a relatively early age.

Cocaine, now I think back to it, was an accident at first. I was fifteen and smoking a spliff in the park, just taking a toke, when someone told me that it had charlie in it. And suddenly, psychosomatically, I felt all far out and scared, because I was sure I'd read somewhere that cocaine rots your brain. For hours afterwards we sat around worrying and saying things like 'My head feels long' to each other. But when you're kids there's not really cocaine around; only movie stars and music industry buffs have access to that sort of stuff. Everything about it – what it was and what it could do to you if you took it – existed in the realms of myth, and I didn't have it again until I was in my twenties and living in London.

The park incident happened at around the same time that I started doing acid and mushrooms, magic ones, of course, that we'd forage for out in the countryside near our estate – a nice way of saying that we went out looking to get high. I was useless at finding mushrooms, so I focused on the acid instead, which was more potent and would take me away for hours. We'd score it from a travellers' site not too far from where we lived, and I became so fond of it that I took it at school a year later. At the time, fractal designs were popping up on posters for raves everywhere; they were really in fashion, and everyone had them covering their exercise books. Four of us had taken these things called Blue Bananas, and I was sitting there in maths completely off my box. How the teacher didn't notice is beyond me. One of my classmates even told him that I was tripping, but he seemed quite oblivious to it. It was so utterly fantastical: I remember just rocking back and forth, the fractals on my exercise books glowing at me. Then I had a drama lesson, a drama exam, in fact, and, given that all I would do was lie on the floor with an office chair and spin it round really slowly, they had to scrap my part in the play. I was absolutely useless, but they had to incorporate me, lying there on the floor, into the play. And I still got away with it.

After a while, acid was all we'd do. Microdots every night to the point where they almost stopped working, and acid and bongs, acid and bongs, acid and bongs below a disused railway line in a long, old tunnel where you never saw the ceiling. It was like being in The Prodigy's 'Firestarter' video. I had an epiphany there once. We were down in the acid tunnel, sitting right in the middle, farthest away from the ends as we always did, with some slightly psychotic older kids who for some reason thought it a good idea to set a motorbike on fire. It must have been the shock absorbers that blew up, because the next thing I was aware of was the most horrific sound, the noise echoing off the walls, and we were confronted with a wall of flame. Everyone else freaked out and ran away – they must have thought Satan had swung by for a bowl – but I didn't move a muscle as pieces of the tank and wheels flew by me, whizzing past and bouncing off the wall. There, in the heart of the explosion, I swear I saw a phoenix rise up and touch the roof, lighting the entire tunnel as it went with a brilliant white light. And, somehow, someone had got up to the curved ceiling and written: 'Pain is an illusion of the senses, fear is an illusion of the mind'. Which means fuck all now, but at fifteen when you're off your face it's pretty profound.

Near-death experiences and brushes with Satan didn't stop us, though. We carried on in the same routine, breaking through the fence into the local trading estate, walking along a wall, fifteen feet high and one brick wide, to steal pallets to break up and burn on our bonfire. Then we used to scramble back and carry them, tripping our balls off, along the brick tightrope and through the fence, carrying them a mile to the acid tunnel in the dark, banging our shins and ankles and stumbling into holes along the way. I once bashed into a burnt-out Ford Capri and started bleeding, my blood appearing green thanks to the acid, and I felt like Jesus with the Cross carrying those things. It was all about the drugs; all we cared about was being totally fucked. Our parents never seemed to notice. It's the same in so many small towns across the country. The smell of the smoke, the paraffin evenings, wrap themselves around my memories of Whitchurch.

When I moved to London, I shed some of the drugs and went straight to booze. I used to drink whatever I could that kept me going, often concoctions such as Diesel – Caffrey's and Stella with vodka and a bit of blackcurrant added. I liked – occasionally still do – a whisky spritzer, too, because the bubbles get you drunk more quickly. When we finally made some money I moved on to imported lager and gin martinis, then David Nivens, which I think were made with brandy and ginger ale; whatever their constituent parts, their name is a delight. Every drink should be called a David Niven. While I was working at the BBC, my girlfriend at the time lived with a girl who was a big clubber, and so little wraps of cocaine would start appearing around her flat. It was a bolt from the blue. I started liking that stuff a lot more than I did back in that park; I liked the coke because if I had more coke I could drink more booze. So I needed the coke, which meant I needed to be around the right people. It's pathetic, but when you start liking a drug it becomes really important. The drug, rather than who you hang out with, is the thing. It's part of the fuzzy logic that drugs give you; it all seems so precise at the time, as if it's the only possible answer.

* * *

Back in the early days of my performing life, I hated going out on stage. I still do. Let me clarify this: I like being there, but that first step over the precipice is a daunting one, and drinking was an encouraging pat on the shoulder, a little pick-me-up to see me across the threshold. I'm not sure when I started asking for Jameson's on our rider, but Jameson's became my thing. It would sit by my monitor patiently as I played the show, its rich blend clinging to the bottle's sides, only disturbed when I took a long, lingering slug. I thought of it as an elegant whiskey, a step-up from Teacher's and Famous Grouse, more cultured somehow. It was a lot more palatable, went down a lot easier than Bell's and it became my drink of choice. My only saving grace is that I've never really been a daytime drinker. That said, a lot of time on tour I'd never slept, so, in my mind, the drink was still part of the event, still ongoing from the night before. That's what I told myself and, thinking back now, I truly believed it. I wasn't trying to hoodwink myself into thinking that I wasn't drinking excessively; I knew I was drinking excessively, I'm just not sure I cared enough to do anything about it. By the end of The Libertines I was easily getting through two bottles of the stuff a day, mostly on my own.

But I'm getting away from myself. For me it was Jameson's Special Reserve, strong continental lager and vodka for the boys and Jack Daniel's for Gary. I was quite haughty about Jack Daniel's: I always thought it a bit of a cliché, though that never stopped me from drinking Jim Beam. I'd drink two bottles of Jameson's and give it little or no respect, and then turn my nose up at a bottle of Jack and consider myself a connoisseur. Like our drinking habits, all our touring habits changed over the years. With The Libertines in those early days when you didn't have your routines, it was a real adventure. You mucked in with everyone, you got your booze and drugs and fags or whatever, whenever or however you could. Whereas, when we'd been going for years, we all had our little rituals, our predictable vices and, strangely enough, it gets boring. It becomes all you do. On those early tours, everything you managed to blag was a treat or a real surprise. The moment when you have your first headline gig, say, and somebody turns up with a packet of something, or you've done a good show so somebody brings you a crate of booze, that's truly thrilling. You feel like you've sung for your supper, even if that supper is a dozen bottles of imported beer.

We started out in the backs of vans, like any band worth its salt, and got promoted to tour buses pretty quickly. That's really when it all started to go a little pear-shaped. When we suddenly had people carrying our equipment, having a crew doing the load-in, that's when the in-fighting started. We became less of a gang and more of a band; it became more of a job. It's a terrible cliché, but success did spoil us. That and the drugs; but they came with the new territory. Inexorably, the magic faded and the routine took over. Whatever we did, it all ended up the same, and for me that meant being drunk through every gig, finishing a bottle during our set and coming off stage and putting away another one. Peter saw that coming before any of us did. He'd rage against the dying light, try to cajole us into not behaving in a linear way. He wanted to break out of the gig/hotel/bus routine very early on, almost as soon as it started happening. 'Don't do that,' he'd say. 'Come on an adventure instead.' And, in a way, he was right, even if that adventure did end in a crackhouse at sunrise.

I remember the first time I saw Peter smoking crack. I hated being around it and I was really furious when I first found out. We were doing demos for Rough Trade in Nomis Studios; he was with a friend of ours and neither of them was doing anything to hide it. I was outraged, along the lines of 'Is that what I think it is?' Desperate questions, and leading to pleading with him not to do it. I remember doing that for a long time. Then I got duped once when I was with Peter and some of his friends. It was raining and it was about seven, maybe eight, in the morning, and they promised we'd find a dealer who'd definitely have some charlie. We got back to the Albion Rooms and someone said that she was on her way. It was an odd hour for a delivery – the lady was supposed to be juggling on the side and to have a nine to five job – but still I was pleased when a little silver Golf with two kids in the back pulled up and a lady got out. She didn't look like a coke dealer, but she gave us two little balloons and disappeared. I went back inside and started cutting it up, but it was like cheese. I wasn't too far gone to think, 'Hang about. This is fucking . . . this isn't what we wanted.' But there was Peter and his mates, already sat in a circle and making a pipe. I'm ashamed to say that I was so pissed, and so intent on getting high, that I sat in there with them and kind of convinced myself that it could have a cocaine feel, the same effect. The pipe came around and, as soon as I'd done it, I instantly wanted more. It was like smoking a bin bag and then having a thirty-second hurry-the-fuck-up panic attack as the pipe moved round the circle, repeating, and then wanting more. Then there were two pipes going around – the other one was the brown to take the edge off the crack – and it was all just so fucking ugly to me. I'd be parachuting, hit the crack and then do the smack to take the edge off. 'It certainly keeps you awake,' they said. I'm lucky I didn't like it, otherwise I'd be dead now for sure. I didn't like it, but when I took it all I ever wanted was more.

I've already mentioned our trip to Paris – the one where we were going to write songs, Peter disappeared across the Continent in pursuit of an ex-girlfriend and I dreamt of my own death night after night. What I didn't mention was the brown we were doing, how we were just doing brown and falling asleep. There were a few times when I thought that if I did it, too, it would draw me closer to Peter. And I kind of hated it, but I was still doing it and I don't know how, but I managed to blag a day to go back to see my then girlfriend at home, and when I tried to drop it casually into the conversation that we'd been doing brown for days she went, quite understandably, fucking ballistic. And that was it: I didn't do it again, ever. If that's being under the thumb then I'm all for it. It was strange; I didn't want to do it, I didn't even like it, yet I was still getting close to actually being hooked on it. Yes, it's costing me money, I don't like it and it's fucked up my life: now just give me a little more.

*   *   *

Looking back on it now, it's easy to see how drugs caused a rift between us. Everything became so serious and emotional; Peter and I would flare up for no reason and there'd be fights and ructions that had never existed before. During the second album recording sessions, Jeff and Michael were there as much to stop us fighting as to stem the flow of drugs into the studio. On day during one of those sessions I remember we fought because I accused him of stealing some money from my sister's room when he burgled my flat. He'd deny it, but then there'd be counter-recriminations, that endless back and forth that happens when a relationship breaks down. To give him his due, I don't think Peter did take her money, but we were on edge all the time. We just wanted to get at each other and I blame the drugs for that.

Drugs took me to the edge with Peter, and the breakdown of my relationship with him, combined with drink, landed me in hospital. This was before the second album sessions, and Peter and I were at Alan McGee's palatial home on the Welsh borders. It was a dark time for the band and for me personally, and Alan, as our manager and friend, was trying his best to heal the rift between Peter and myself, to make us whole again. Though we did manage to make merry a little, it was a tough time, lots of talking late into the night, analysing what had gone wrong between us, why Peter had kicked in my door on Harley Street and tried to take my stuff – little things like that. We'd set out from London with high hopes, with the intention of writing some new songs, but now I can see that we were getting ahead of ourselves with that idea. There was too much between us to go straight back to writing music together. But I admire Alan for coming up with the idea, and, later, some songs did surface that had had their genesis in that period. One night at Alan's it got too much and we all got too drunk and I was angry with Peter but, rather than direct it at him physically, because I'm just not like that, I retreated to the bathroom while he retreated to his bedroom. I stood in the bathroom and looked at myself for a long time in the mirror not quite sure what I was seeing, and then began to smash my head over and over again into the basin; then, and I've no idea how, I managed to get myself into bed.

The next morning I woke up not quite knowing what was going on. My entire head was numb, and I couldn't really see, but there was a trail of blood leading from the bed towards the bathroom, and the bed itself, sheets, duvets, pillows and headboard, was liberally splashed with scarlet; it was like someone had tipped a tin of red paint over everything. I must have lost pints. I went downstairs and Alan was sitting down, talking on the phone, and he did a double take before slamming down the receiver. I think he thought at first that I was playing a practical joke, wearing some Halloween mask to scare him; mask or not, I think I managed that. It wasn't something that was new to me. There had been times in the past when, less dramatically, I'd get drunk and emotional and head-butt walls and knock myself out. In all honesty, it was usually when there were people around, so they could react, be horrified, tell me how crazy I was and offer to look after me. Girls, usually. But the basin was much worse. I think it was a signal for help, that I needed to be rescued.

That rescue didn't happen for a long time, though; not even a complete ban on drinking could do it. The ban came after the Moscow trip, at the tail end of Dirty Pretty Things. It was no surprise – it wasn't as if I was just looking a little washed out, just feeling a bit under the weather. The oncoming pancreatitis was making me feel like my insides were exploding. We'd practically been living on gear and I was eating handfuls of steroids a day just to keep me balanced and to clear my head. I was doing so much coke that I couldn't breathe through my nose. There's nothing more miserable than a person who's trying to do coke but who is actually just pushing powder around a plate with a straw because he can't breathe properly. We were downing huge tumblers of Russian vodka, then I'd attempt to snort a line and throw six of these red pills down my neck, decongestants of some sort. At least I think that's what they were. I used to go to see the doctor all the time, especially after a cocaine binge, and tell him that I had a dust allergy or hay fever. No one's going to believe me if I ever get hay fever again.

Back from Moscow, the pain didn't stop, but neither did it stop me. I remember how it shot through me, having a meeting in a pub and having a glass of wine; all sorts of situations, and the thought that it might return would make me panic. Later on I'd try a beer, and panic-thinking it was all going to happen again. Then I had an interview with a *Scottish Mirror* journalist, who came to see me in the studio and couldn't stop wincing. Even when I talked I was in pain, and the article the next day mentioned how Carl had struggled valiantly on. That didn't make any difference to me, though: another visit to the doctor, some more tablets, but they did nothing – like hay fever pills for a cocaine addiction. Only when a friend came round to see me did I finally buckle and give way. He'd come to talk about the breakdown of his relationship with his girlfriend and left with me beside him in a taxi destined for hospital. This is going to sound ridiculous coming from someone who cared so little about his health, but I had health insurance. And so I lay there in my private room with the reassuring sounds of London traffic far below, light streaming in misty rays through the window, the TV on quietly and the morphine taking me away to some undiluted place, uncaring, just happily off my head as my body healed.

Then came the crushing news that I couldn't drink any more. Professional opinions differed. Some people told me that I'd never drink again, and at that news my stomach flipped over, just as it had when I was lost and homeless in the Parisian night and had reached into my back pocket to discover my passport was missing. Others said I should cut it out for a year, and then I'd be restricted to one beer, that sort of thing. But after three months of not drinking I decided to try again. I had one beer in Brazil, the beach was below me, the view white sand and endless sky, as I squinted at the label and put the cold bottle to my lips. The skin on my shoulders was a reddish-brown that was already beginning to peel, and I was wearing a straw hat – strange, the things you remember. The beer felt vital and good as it made its cold passage towards my belly, and I think I held the bottle up reverentially against the light, admiring its shape and feeling good about things again. Within hours, however, the pain was back, bolting through my stomach and up my side.

I persevered with drinking, though, like the idiot I am. I won't try to make excuses for my inability not to drink, but it's very, very unpleasant to live the life I was living without boozing. When you're sober it gets to eleven o'clock and suddenly everyone's got bad breath, everyone's talking right in your face and repeating themselves, not listening to a word you say. Which, of course, is exactly who you are, I am, everybody is, when you're hammered. That was Billy Connolly's take on things: he said the reason he stopped going to the pub with his mates after he'd cleaned up and stopped drinking was because he realised how dull his friends were, and how dull he was, when they were pissed. I noticed exactly the same thing. Why does nobody understand personal space? I have since been told that I've made a full recovery, my internals are as they should be and I can now drink normally again – whatever that means.

Famously, or perhaps infamously, drugs were The Libertines' springboard, crutch and stumbling block – beginning, middle and end – but they played a generous part in Dirty Pretty Things' decline, too. As I mentioned, the coke we had in the studio for our second album turned out to be laced very generously with crystal meth. The studio's enough of a boiler room as it is, but with chemically induced paranoia there were bound to be fireworks – and not the wonderful bursts of light that fill an autumn night sky. So we fought endlessly. Fighting is usually anathema to me – I go out of my way to avoid it – but due to the crystal meth coke I wasn't backing down. I remember raised voices, thrown punches. We wrestled as far as I can recall – which isn't very far. It was all very *Women in Love*. Though can I at this point exonerate Gary, our drummer? He never seemed to touch any drug, so when we would all be raging and fighting, he'd fall straight to sleep – a trick I wish I could have learnt. I was talking to a therapist about this (more of whom later) and he said it sounded as if the band was dead, and that, by that point, I wanted it to be that way. I think he was right: even then, I realized subconsciously that I couldn't stay with Dirty Pretty Things. There was too much bullshit. The pain and angst outweighed everything, and I hadn't got into another band just to have to deal with all the same crap again. So I disbanded, put a stop to it and it eventually turned out all right.

* * *

Up until recently I still had the hangover from my lifestyle on the road: sleeping only three nights a week, with a lack of purpose and of direction to boot. And, on top of the lack of direction, I wanted to do it. They're glamorous, drink and drugs; there's no point in denying it. They helped me walk tall, yet they also laid me very low. They did for both my bands and wrecked the friendship I had with Peter. Sadly, none of that ever stopped me.

Red wine and tea have fuelled this book, as they have my music. If I reached out a hand now I could grab a glass and drain it, just as I used to with Jameson's whiskey, my long-time friend and on-stage collaborator. But I don't need to. Red wine is safer, somehow. When did it all change? After Dirty Pretty Things, it took me a long time to work out that the drink and the drugs and the sex were a dead end. What it took was therapy, a woman and seven days without sleep, the longest week of my life, to push me beyond, to bring some peace to something inside me. Now that I'm getting on with other stuff, working on a new album, recruiting a band, writing songs, living with my girlfriend, drugs aren't a problem. My girlfriend doesn't like me on coke. Strangely, I don't like me on coke now, either. I'm over thirty, and I actually like going to bed. I sleep at night and I like eating. And if, every now and then, at four in the morning I think it's a great idea to do some more gear, the feeling of wanting to pull my own skin off the next day is a stiff reminder of why I should lay off it.

I was scared in the park that time I was fifteen and I realized I'd taken it, and maybe I should have heeded the warning there and then. But I don't blame my teenage self: he'd keep on making mistakes for at least another fifteen years. The drink and the drugs were just part of the journey.

TEN

Of Kickboxing and Crystals

Some people say good songs come out of depression, that art needs angst, but not for me it doesn't. For me it can only come out of really feeling life and feeling alive. Only with a bolt of some kind of vital divinity do I even begin to think about the songwriting process, so, for me, the depression is when that can't happen. And, after Dirty Pretty Things, everything stopped. I had a lost season, a period of consumption and excess – a time full of nothing. I felt like I'd left Dirty Pretty Things with a good heart, although I was sad at how things had become, and I'd learnt a few lessons from it: don't be a lazy shit; follow your heart; don't invite Miguel into the studio; don't try to write twelve 'Bang Bang's, and for fuck's sake be strong. Summer quickly faded, Christmas came and went and I realized that I was creatively fallow, a vacuum. Looking back now, I think I was getting rid of all the chaff and waiting for reality to come, but that wasn't how it felt at the time. It was at this point that I turned to a therapist for help. That was one of the things that set me back on my feet.

I'd been in therapy before Dirty Pretty Things split, although I'd always been mistrustful of it – I felt it was all about old couches and old men, weakness and failure. But my first foray into therapy – the first time I felt myself going under – was just after Peter had gone to prison. I was still living up on Harley Street, probably getting my front door fixed, drinking myself to sleep, and barely crawling out of bed when I was awake. I felt I was dragging a dead weight around with me everywhere I went, and a friend – someone who has seen me through thick and thin, who has shown a lot of heart – recommended a person I should visit. Even though I perceived it to be some sort of freak show, I was so desperate and unhappy that a part of me wanted in. The therapist, who pretty much lived up to all my worst expectations, told me to stop drinking and doing drugs and suggested the twelve-step programme. I remember my reaction as being something like: *That's not my problem: my problem is depression, what are you talking about?* Subsequently, I've realized that stopping the substance use is a recurring, and correct, piece of advice. It's taken me a long time to acknowledge the truth of it, but if I don't take loads of drink and drugs, then I don't get anywhere near as depressed. I do still get depressed – it's part of who I am – but without those things it's a lot easier to live with. However, twelve steps wasn't a life choice I wanted to make, so I only visited that therapist twice. I wasn't getting the answers I wanted to hear (I'm aware of how ludicrous that sounds), and because it was so rigid and uptight – all leather chairs and bronze dog sculptures, note-taking and 'Tell me about your mother' – I just didn't see for a second how it was going to help me. I decided I was just too busy drinking to go again.

Would things have turned out differently if I'd gone on a different day, with a different mindset, or if any one of a thousand variables had been different? I still ask myself that, because, after I decided not to go back, I just went mad. I drank and drugged my way through two bands: you only have to look at the chapter on Dirty Pretty Things to see how hell bent I was on self-destruction. I look at the situations we put ourselves in and wonder if that was in any way deliberate: was I subconsciously trying to push some sort of button? The next brush with therapy came during Dirty Pretty Things, between albums, although the band did seem in limbo, in some sort of holding pattern, sort of running out of fuel. It was after I'd taken up kickboxing. Someone in our management had encouraged the whole band to do it – kickboxing, that is, not therapy – and everyone else had decided not to. I, however, went along with it, imagining that practising that kind of physical art form would be a release, that the emotion would pour out of me, but in the event I could be furious and it would all just sit inside me, buzzing around my chest, unable to flow out through my limbs. I could never make that little hole in the dam, to begin the little trickle that would eventually let everything flood out. Afterwards, I'd be knackered, frustrated and really upset; I had no release. I was kickboxing on my own, just going in with a hangover every day, three times a week, and, in the end, the kickboxing just tailed off. I was asked to compete, but I missed the weigh-in because I had a hangover. That just about summed everything up. I gave it up. I'd been hit in the face enough, and my heart was no longer in it. After that, I slumped. I knew that if I even went for a walk I'd feel great, but I couldn't even muster the energy to get up and leave the house. Some of the band were trying to talk me around at that point, to get me interested in some songs they were working on, but I was useless. On top of it all, our management problems – it was splintering apart – were looking to me more and more like a prelude to the band's own demise. I had the black dog on my shoulder and I was starting to have real problems with my girlfriend. I can't imagine my state of mind helped: I must have been as much fun to be around as a box of broken glass. So I screwed up my courage and rang another therapist, dressing my case up a little to make sure he'd agree to see me – probably symptomatic of how messed up I was. No wonder I spent six months trying to kick other people.

These days, I consider the man, my second therapist, a good, insightful friend, but at the time I couldn't help feeling that he was meddling in my life – in a lot of people's lives, actually. The real reason I stopped seeing him, though, was because of a retreat he took me on. It struck him as a profound idea, given my upbringing bouncing from hippy communes to a working-class home like a demented ping-pong ball, and so, when he suggested it, I agreed. I'm not sure what I was expecting. Maybe a cottage in the Cotswolds or on the Welsh borders; picture windows and rolling hills; groups of us sitting around in big, battered armchairs. A cat, maybe, but definitely some clarity to my thinking, so I was as surprised as anyone to find myself in the departure lounge at Heathrow. I wondered if it was too early to get a drink and whether, if I did get a drink, it would be frowned upon to offer him one. (As it turned out, I wouldn't be allowed a drop for the duration of the trip.) A couple of hours later we touched down in northern Spain and drove to what I can only describe as a hippy commune. The reality of the commune was a shock to my system. In the vein of juggling and fire-breathing, unicycling and poys, unappealing nudism and rebirthing ceremonies aided by crystals: all the dark arts were being practised. I took part in yoga sessions, which were interesting and very hard work (although I missed the kicking aspect of my exercise regime), tried to avoid the preponderance of crystal-based energy ceremonies, and chomped my way unenthusiastically through the tasteless vegan dinners sourced entirely from the commune's grounds. The sessions with the therapist were good, but otherwise I couldn't escape the feeling that I'd walked straight back into my childhood, something like the film *Westworld*, in which punters paid to immerse themselves in a past reality, only without the fun bits – Yul Brynner, Stetsons and robot hookers. My face ached from all the wincing I did and physically I was on edge. I realized I had to get home: I had to face up to problems on my own.

My grandfather passing away while I was at the retreat was the catalyst to leaving – the David Niven grandfather, the grandfather whom I idolized. I left the commune not cleansed, not reborn, simply at a loss, and guilty that I hadn't been able to say goodbye to my grandfather, or to be with him when he died. Until his funeral I was an utter mess, though my family came together in the worst of circumstances, and I tried to help my grandmother out. She'd just lost her partner of sixty-five years, which made the Spanish retreat pale into insignificance.

* * *

I saw the therapist a few more times after Spain, and the mists began to clear. I began to take stock of things, and to come to terms with the path my performing life had taken me down. My gigging life had started at the age of sixteen and, from that band's very first gig – we only did three – I was absolutely petrified with stage fright. It was at a pub called the Railway in Winchester, and I wasn't singing, just concentrating on hiding behind my guitar, using it as a weapon to deflect the gaze of the people – the few there were – staring up at us. Even so, the nerves were just awful. Our second gig was worse, because we'd got rid of the singer – he really couldn't sing, though he remains a good friend – and I'd taken on vocal duties, pushed up there to the front with my mouth open, thinking, *How and why am I here?* It was like I'd been scooped up by a tornado and deposited miles away from normality. It might sound ludicrous now, but that's how alien it all felt. And to this day when I'm on stage I still find myself thinking, *What have I done in my life to end up here?* Someone once told me how cocky and comfortable I looked up on stage and I thought, *You've really got no idea.*

It was Peter who taught me to stand up on a stage and helped me to master – if not conquer – the fright that still paralyses me when I'm waiting to perform, and I thank him for that. Together, we used to roll around playing all sorts of bits and bobs wherever we could. We'd see a poster outside a pub advertising for performers, for instance, and troop right in there. We'd do open mic nights and I couldn't enjoy them, mostly because the standard was usually pretty dire; the second reason was the dreaded words 'Right, you're up next'. One minute I'd be sitting there finding something to stare at on the floor, my stomach doing loops, filled with the absolute fear of God, thinking of ways to get out of it. The next I'd be bolt upright saying, 'Oh my guitar's out of tune', or 'I suddenly feel sick', and then I'd flee. I'd catch Peter's eye as I was heading out of the door and he'd look at me as if to say, *What the fucking hell are you doing?* and I'd stand in the street smoking a cigarette, like a condemned man on his final fag. I've never got over it, this weird brand of stage terror. I often ask myself why the hell I've chosen this life as a performer, but I owe it to Peter: I could never have done it without him. He opened up that bit of me.

I also learnt to forgive those fans who would try and keep me in the past. I did an *NME* cover with Morrissey once, and Morrissey said, 'To some people I'll always be Morrissey from The Smiths, no matter what else I do. And you'll always be Carl from The Libertines.' I've never minded that, I'm proud of it; what I've had trouble with, though, are the ghoulish people who thrive on the darkness they imagine exists between Peter and me, running back and forth trying to make our business their business, carrying poisoned *bons mots* toward me like apples spiked with razors on Halloween, and inviting me to eat. The strangers who order me to sort it out, faces close to mine, leering, 'Get back together with Pete.' I remember visiting Peter once at his flat, after he came to that Dirty Pretty Things gig in Paris, and it was full of people whispering about us, brown tinfoil poking out of their pockets, staring across the room and imagining scenarios between us, hooked on a long-dead idea of The Libertines, an idea that disintegrated when Peter and me did finally speak. Because, when we do, all of that crap becomes totally insignificant. People often used to tell me 'Pete thinks this . . .' and 'Pete thinks that . . .', but, because he was my best mate, my dearest friend, I always had an idea what he was thinking. We're not going to lose that, though we've both moved on. We both had to. And that's why, I think, I never saw the girls on Brighton Pier's lack of interest in Dirty Pretty Things as a low point. It was just something to accept. The moment happens, and then it's gone.

* * *

It's late at night again, and I'm half a bottle of wine down. Maybe it's that, or maybe it's looking back at what I've left behind, but I've started to notice certain things. The realization that, although you can still stomach twelve pints, and then some, the first bit of alcohol in the evening does change you. Hands getting older, tiredness edges around the eyes; and you realize that's mortality talking. Also, in truth, my family-to-be has provoked a certain reassessment.

I still go back to those early days in north London, down those back alleys of my mind, to when we were ambitious, bright, undaunted – or that's how I see The Libertines as we walk through Kentish Town, on our way to rehearse down on Patshull Road, where John's mum lives, walking up from there to the swimming ponds at Hampstead Heath, where Peter would always insist on wearing his seventies-style, brightly coloured flannel Speedos. I've left Camden now, but I'm not too far away. I visit often, and my heart's still there. I'm not such an idiot as to romanticize Camden and Kentish Town, or even London, out of all proportion, but sometimes I'll sit out in the sunshine and sip a coffee, and I'll see Peter go by in his pornographic swimming trunks, Natasha ducking into a cab on the Holloway Road with the light hurting her eyes, Max lamping some students, Rock Paul drinking his cancer away, or me and Johnny clambering over a gate to get to the South Bank and watch the new millennium arrive. Then, suddenly, there I am, fifteen and stepping off the train at Waterloo looking up at London's skyline with wide eyes. I hope I never stop seeing it like that.

ELEVEN

Pushing On

It's a common desire, perhaps, but all I ever wanted was to be a singer in a band. Unlike many, I was lucky enough to achieve that desire, but I was also doomed to destroy it for myself: everything within these pages, everything I've discovered about myself and the way I work best are proof positive that it's best I work alone. It makes me sad that I'm not part of a band: I never wanted to do this on my own. It doesn't take the keenest analytical mind to assess my childhood, divided between bricks and mortar, and canvas beneath the stars, and realize that all I ever wanted was to belong. And, given that I lost a twin brother, no surprise that I was looking for a band of brothers, or that I bonded so closely with Peter in The Libertines or with Anthony in Dirty Pretty Things. My lack of confidence in myself is clear now for me to see, but I think it was the final album sessions with Dirty Pretty Things that made me realize how much I lacked confidence in my own songwriting abilities, too. I deliberately distract myself in case I can't manage the job at hand, and after The Libertines and

Dirty Pretty Things I realized that when I've got someone to hide behind I tend not to do anything. Procrastination is the thief of time, said Edward Young. That should be my next tattoo. Sometimes I think I need a metaphorical Peter running in to my imaginary Old Vic and screaming in my face 'We're meant to be writing!' every time I get the urge to go and do something else instead. Okay, maybe not that, but you get the picture. Little by little, I've learnt to deal with the self-sabotage, but going it alone, which I realized was what I had to do, is still terrifying.

* * *

When you jump overboard, or your ship sinks, you either go under or you strike out for shore. In January 2009, I found myself coming in to land at LAX, determined to make it to dry land cleansed of my sins rather than lose myself in the choppy waters. I'd arranged some low-key solo gigs supporting Glasvegas on their US tour, my first time performing before an audience since the breakdown of Dirty Pretty Things. Frogmarching myself over there to face down my demons did, however, seem increasingly foolish as the itchy fingers of fear clutched at me in the immigration line. I had no visa, a support tour to complete and a complicated story to tell the stony-faced official awaiting me, something vague about a road trip to visit multiple friends on the West Coast. I'd made up names and locations on the aeroplane, filled in forms in the airport and felt sweat forming on my neck even in the icy, air-conditioned interior of the arrivals hall. Finally, I handed them in, to be waved through, without realizing they'd been marked to make sure I was checked out. I was pulled aside and left in a room and, even though I'd sent my guitar on ahead, grilled about my luggage. I think my line about visiting Joshua Tree National Park, which somewhere over the Atlantic had occurred to me as a nice conversational aside, simply caused them to furrow their brows and jot something down in their notebooks. I was scared stiff, waiting for one of them to disappear from the room and come back with a page he'd Googled and printed off, my grinning face peering out from a darkened stage somewhere, my fate sealed, my seat on the next plane home booked.

It got little better when they let me through: I felt like a man heading for the gallows as I walked on stage at LA's Troubadour that night. I was convinced I was going to be found out. I had a set list of songs that I'd been playing for years, songs for which, even in my blurriest states, my fingers had reliably found the complicated patterns on the fretboard and my mouth the requisite shapes to sing the words. Still a question hung over me: what the fuck was I doing there? There was an element of preaching to the converted, which was welcome, but I had something to prove to myself – because if I don't feel challenged then I go the other way and all hell breaks loose. I felt alternately ashamed, hopeful and scared. It goes back to Michael Gambon's question: 'What is your purpose?'

What was my purpose? Glasvegas dropped me off in LA and we parted on good terms, even though I'd perhaps thrown one too many parties on their bus. I was at a loose end. Glasvegas had gone home and I didn't really care for that idea, and, besides, I had a few meetings that my dear friend Chris McCormack had set up. Chris knew people: in fact, he seemed to know everyone. He is the ex-guitarist from 3 Colours Red, a band that were Camden icons in the late nineties. We met in Japan towards the end of a Libertines tour, and we've been friends ever since. With his spiky hair and leather jacket, Geordie accent, plethora of tattoos and unrivaled tolerance to narcotics and alcohol, it was safe to say that we instantly got on well. I'd been looking in to writing songs for commercials – I needed the money, but mostly I needed something to do. I needed guidelines. Chris had some meetings organized, why didn't I attend those meetings, too? He made his way to town and all hell broke loose. In California, you can stay out on the streets at night and not get cold. That thought occurred to me on the Strip one boozy, boozy night. It wasn't profound and it certainly wasn't clear-headed, but after roughing it in both London and Paris it seemed important to know that, if the unthinkable happened or if I simply got lost and couldn't find my way back to our apartment, I wouldn't freeze. In the middle of the mayhem we did some pitches, which I doubt we impressed in, and then Har Mar Superstar came round. We greeted him like an old friend, primarily because he is an old friend; he set up his video camera and said he wanted to make a show. There are many things to see and do on the internet, so I won't be offended if you don't take the time to track down *Two British Dudes*. It's pretty crap: just me off my head playing myself twice in a little sketch. The only possible point of interest is that you can gauge how intense our partying had become. I'd been awake for two nights at that point, I'm ghostly white and have disastrously dirty teeth. God only knows what the two women who were meant to be taking us to our appointments from our villa on Sunset thought when they came to get us each morning, if we were even there at all.

We didn't pick up any advertising work in LA as far as I remember, and flew out of the city, two sloppy Englishmen on the last scheduled flight out, asleep before take-off, only coming to, dry-mouthed, over Manhattan, with barely time for a drink before we landed. The snow clung to our coats and hair as we queued for a cab, the wind pushing us around a bit. We were here for yet more meetings, but I didn't care. It was just a convenient excuse not to go home and face up to whatever was next. We were staying up in Harlem, where we instantly slid into a bar, to beat the New York gales and to watch Barack Obama's inauguration. I sat and watched him trip up over his lines, and was glad to see he was human like the rest of us, even if I was feeling anything but. I looked around the bar and wondered what the people sitting there must have thought, if they really believed he could save them, if he could clean the tarnish left by the Bush years.

The New York ad agencies were worse than in LA. I understood there'd be financial benefits to the job, but within an hour of being in those offices I thought, *I can't do this. This is horrible.* I mean no offence to people who actually make adverts for a living. It takes a lot of discipline. It just wasn't me. Writing to spec, composing music to which an actor-model could be seen miming some horrific jingle . . . I loathed myself enough as it was. I couldn't have done that – and that was when I assumed it was easy money at which I could turn my nose up. It turned out that it wasn't easy money at all. The ad

pitches we did were endless, arduous work and, at the end of it –
nothing. Not even a call-back. The pitch was for Lincoln Town Cars,
as far as I can recall, the sort of car we'd often have picking us up at
the airport when we travelled as a band. They're big old things, with
room enough for two or three bodies in the trunk even after you've
put your suitcases in. And that was it for New York. Bodies in the
trunk, rejection by Lincoln Town Cars and the wind cutting through
you on the avenues. I remember thinking it would be no place to
grow old. All the cocaine and whisky had affected my mood.

I lurched through the spring like a drunk lurching through a pub
door, looking a bit like Ray Milland in *The Lost Weekend* – ironic,
as I'd left New York by then. It was still cold in London: not New
York cold, but enough of an excuse to go from home to the pub and
then back again. As the thaw came I began to feel ill and empty, and
the house was ghoulish and abandoned in the stark spring light. It
looked like I felt on the inside: clutter and crap everywhere, no care
taken. I began to put the dirty dishes in the cupboards where they'd
once been stored clean, obsessively hiding things in pizza boxes, and
barely ventured out of the front door. I was becoming reclusive, like
Howard Hughes, but unlike Hughes I wasn't even close to being a
millionaire, and didn't seem to mind the dirt at all.

* * *

I had to set about challenging myself again, and this time I found
myself on an industrial estate in South Wimbledon, learning how to
lasso and to speak with an American accent. I was to star in a new
production of *Fool for Love*, a Sam Shepard play, opposite Sadie Frost.

I was hoping that my training as an actor, the bit after the drama exam on LSD but before meeting Peter and forming The Libertines, would stand me in good stead.

I'd been introduced to Sadie Frost back when I was still sofa-surfing around London, by Danny Goffey of Supergrass. I remember the first evening, when Danny, now an old friend, and I had walked from the Dublin Castle back to the house Sadie shared with Jude Law, Guinness and black in hand, and I'd made myself comfortable at the upright piano that was set against one wall, out of the way of the rest of the party. I was a little intimidated as it was my first contact with that 'celebrity' circle. I placed my drink down on top of it, only to discover that the lid was up. The glass disappeared out of sight with a crunching sound, and purply black liquid started oozing through the keys. I quickly checked that no one was watching, quietly closed the lid and moved across the room to prepare myself another drink.

Danny and I sat up all that night back at his, playing the guitar and watching Supergrass videos until the sun came up – something that never fails to surprise me – and we walked out into the diluted sunshine looking for an off-licence where we bought some champagne. We didn't have a plan – actually, there was the usual plan: keep on drinking – but I loped along, the champagne clinking softly in the bag, until I tripped and fell, and a bottle shattered. We didn't have a clue what to do, so we went back to the shop and tried to persuade the shopkeeper that the bottle had exploded of its own volition, convinced that he'd buy our story until he threatened to throw us out of the shop, so we stood in the street, the morning dreamlike and soft around the edges, wondering whether to buy more or simply to go home. Then Danny leant forward, one hand placed gently on my cheek, and pulled a long shard of glass out of my head in one sharp motion. I forget whether or not it hurt.

I always quite fancied myself as a trained actor, and, after a few drinks, wasn't shy about telling people just that. I also have a purist's, and a possibly misplaced, idea that everyone's got an actor in them, so, when Sadie called out of the blue to ask me about the play I thought, *Well, I've always talked the talk and I usually try and punish myself at least once a year.* Sam Shepard's *Fool for Love* seemed as good a way to crucify myself as any. We travelled together down to rehearsals, probably the first time Sadie had used the Tube for twenty years. She turned up, the first day, in a big hat and sunglasses. I think she assumed everyone in the carriage was going to pounce on her. Nobody batted an eyelid. We were on the Tube together again the day the *Evening Standard* published a piece on the play, accompanied by a photo of the pair of us spread across two pages; there we were, sitting together, and no one even looked up. You have to admire London commuters' dedication to getting from A to B while steadfastly ignoring everything around them.

It was a real pleasure working with Sadie, who is a sweet and generous person. Somehow, I felt instantly comfortable with her on stage. Before rehearsals started, I knew nothing about Shepard, until someone told me he was America's Shakespeare. At which point I started to tremble, and redoubled my efforts. When we opened, the reviews accused me of not knowing the script, but I don't think that was the problem. I knew the lines, but didn't understand the words sufficiently to convey them convincingly. I could perform them parrot fashion, but I wrestled with the subtext, and didn't make real sense of it until we were well into our three-month run. I'd sit backstage waiting to go on and the phrase 'baptism of fire' would run around the walls of my head until the bell rang and someone called me to the stage.

All in all, I think the theatre was more frightening that my first film experience, which had happened some time earlier. I'd been to see *Telstar* when the play was on its West End run, and had thought it remarkable – a play that, in fact, I must have talked up in the press because, in the same unexpected manner as Sadie would later call, I received a surprise letter from Nick Moran, who co-wrote the play, thanking me for saying such lovely things about it and asking me if I'd be interested in playing Gene Vincent in the movie version he was to be directing. I went to meet Nick and was instantly mesmerized by Shepperton Studios, a true, childlike awe, then went away and immersed myself in Gene Vincent's world. I sat up nights, a bottle of red wine at my side, watching the flickering images of him driving the young women of his generation wild. He looked like a hero, and I practised and practised his style. I even had his limp down.

In the film world everyone jumps up out of bed and is on set at 6 a.m., where they then stand around for hours while the doors of static caravans open and close and a few select people walk about purposefully. The waiting process did nothing for my nervousness. I remember pulling Nick aside to outline my approach and voice some dramatic concerns; he levelled his gaze at me and told me to get on set, say my one line and then get off again. When the time came, I stood there like a rabbit in the headlights and mumbled something about looking for the toilet, repeated it once, and that was it. I don't think I did the best job I could have done but it was certainly an eye-opener. You spend a quarter or a third of a year working on a play and, by its close, really understand what you're doing – at which point, the performance is lost in the annals of memory. On the other hand, my grandchildren will be able to look up *Telstar* online and no doubt marvel at my dodgy clip.

Later, in the darkness of the Leicester Square cinema, I peered up at my face, six feet wide on the screen, my only thought something banal about how my hair had fallen down. My lustrous Gene Vincent quiff looked little more than an inglorious bowl cut. I looked like a redneck, I thought, all buck teeth and pudding basin hairdo. I glanced along the row of seats at the rest of the cast and sunk progressively lower into the plush velvet, until, when the lights came up, I realized that it was all right, that no one was staring at me. I'd got away with it – how I feel about a lot of my gigs. Overall, I was more pleased with the performance bits than I was with my lines. Even if I did only mime (and, to be honest, I hadn't been sure of the words), I did that whole Vincent thing: the hand obscuring the mouth, over the microphone. If I ever act again, I'll be sure not to read the reviews, because, even though they were mainly positive, every now and again a line floats back to me, something some no-mark said about ruining Gene Vincent for him. But then everyone's a critic, aren't they?

* * *

Gradually, as I put some distance between me and my bands, as I challenged and extended myself into new areas, my songwriting began to blossom once again. I'd kept on writing all the way through, automatically, because that's what I did and I didn't know anything else.

I found the freedom to write on my own liberating. You kid yourself that you can do what you like with your songs in a band, but for me at least that wasn't true. On my own, I began to write about the things that were important which never tied in with any band I've been in. And after a while, the songs had started to coalesce, to take shape around certain ideas. I tried a different palate, things I never would have got away with in a band – and gave myself the opportunity to play some fairly patchy piano, for starters. Sitting there, looking out over the leafy suburbs of north London, trilling away at the keys, I felt a sense of calm, that I'd connected to something I hadn't before. I took a lot of the guitars away just to see what I might come up with, without reverting to the same old crash, bang, wallop format. A part of me needed to be naked I guess, but try walking into a rehearsal room and telling these expectant faces that you've been working on some new material and then plonking yourself down at a piano and start a profound lament about the dark beauty of human frailty.

I jest, or at least in part, because I think there's a lot more humour in my songs now. My songwriting lost its humour during The Libertines – suddenly an early song like 'The Boys In The Band' was frowned upon because The Libertines became such a serious thing. From a certain point on, in The Libertines, or in Dirty Pretty Things, I tried to keep it all lofty, to hide the truth away. It was almost as if humour wasn't allowed, only anger and bitterness – which was a tragedy, given where we'd come from. I think the first song I wrote that appears on the album is a ballad called 'So Long My Lover, It's Over', which for me is pretty much the only link to the past. Elsewhere, there's a bit of lightness back with this record.

* * *

It took me a while to find my voice solo, to realize what it was I was writing about, and I still find it much easier to write for other people. I did two songs for *Get Him to the Greek*, Russell Brand's film, and took a short trip to LA to play in his live band. For the soundtrack work the brief simply said one was to be about love, and the other was a party song. That set me on the back foot a bit – I like a bit of direction – and the party song's chorus ('Let's get fucked, let's get fucked, let's get fucked up . . .') won't be winning me an Ivor Novello Award any time soon.

It was during that soundtrack work that Edie came along and saved me. I was working on a session in south London, and had been keeping my eye out for a cellist for Russell Brand's songs. I liked the way she looked through the control room glass, I liked the way she played, and she told me she sang, too, though she also told me about her boyfriend. She played on the recordings I did for *Get Him to the*

Greek, and I sent the demos over, as a first sketch, and, despite their simplicity, the film-makers loved them – at which point I did, too. What was odd was that I'd only sent them over as a prototype, simply to ask 'Is this the right direction?' It had always been the intention to re-record them in LA, and both songs, in spruced-up versions, made the final cut. I was touched.

Edie and I became friends, and I used her for a gig up in Scotland – it was a solo gig I'd been planning for a while, my first in the UK, and suddenly it seemed important to factor in some strings to make it work. She was a person who, just by her presence, would make me happy, though I also felt a magnetic attraction. I thought about her a lot during my seven days awake, the longest week of my life, and she was undoubtedly a beacon who helped me make it through that, but all the while we remained friends and friends only. She was very loyal to her boyfriend, which I respected, and was surprised at myself for doing so. Given my past history with women, during which I'd often shown scant regard for any of the proprieties of normal relationships, I wouldn't have paid his feelings – or hers, for that matter – a second thought. But even to have her in my life, as a friend, seemed to quieten something in me, and keep my trust issues and fear of abandonment at bay. When they separated, finally, she came round to watch a DVD, and we had our first kiss over popcorn. From then on, everything else just faded into the background, and all the noise that had surrounded me for so long was suddenly silent.

Life with Edie had a purpose. She didn't like me being too wrecked, and I found that I didn't like myself like that either. Also, as I've said, I've never been truly creative in that state, so thanks to her I began to be able to work and write again. I had someone to give my love to, and it healed me. Soon after Edie and I started going out, I went to see another therapist, because I was worried that I was embarking on this whole new thing and that my new girlfriend might be thinking I'm a fucking old depressive. I was also performing in *Fool for Love*, and had taken to having a quiet beer each night after the play, a quiet beer that had turned into several raucous ones, and I was worried I was heading down that road again. The therapist came to see the play, and we met several times, painful, agonizing sessions where it felt as if I was on the rack, laid bare. They'd hurt me for weeks after, and I do feel some catharsis from them.

The therapist also helped me through my fears over getting The Libertines back together. I was in the British Library, looking for John Lennon's lyrics and wondering why they weren't housed there any more, when I got the telephone call offering a re-formed Libertines some live festival shows. To have received the offer in a place so full of grandeur, literature and history seemed like a good omen. And thinking of the British Library also takes me back to my early days in town, when I worked for a time at the British Museum, which housed the British Library's books long before I came on the scene. The job at the British Museum came with privileged access to areas of the museum that were closed to the public. Behind closed doors I got to look under great grey drapes covering ancient pieces of marble, and be completely alone in the gathering stillness, just me and huge chunks of history. It could be overwhelming. I was living with some of my mum's friends in Dulwich and each day I'd put on my suit and get a taxi into work. The cabs there and back would cost me half a day's wages but I was working in London at the British Museum: naturally I had to wear a suit and travel in a black cab. Why else would I have moved there? Somehow, re-forming the band seemed to connect with that optimism and romance once again, and to be looking for Lennon's lyrics, connecting with English music's Arcadian past, seemed just right, too.

* * *

I always used to fret when journalists asked me to pin down the specifics of what I write about. I suppose I'm scared that if you pull out the keystone then the whole edifice collapses. So I tell them that all I can ever do is tell the truth through my eyes, and put it out there in the vague hope that it connects with somebody else. That's the point at which they tend to look down at their notes and ask me about the red jackets we used to wear. These days, now I've settled down, my songs are all caught up in my family. I'm still a creature of chance, and of jeopardy, and it could be that the biggest risks and biggest successes – personally and creatively – are still to come. But now I'm standing on the edge of the precipice hand in hand with a lady that loves me, and a family to be part of. For a while recently, my grandfather (not the David Niven one) was in hospital and, coupled with the baby, it made me fret that I'd start writing like Elton John – late, 'Circle of Life' Elton John, not the good seventies stuff. Doctors and nurses look at me less gravely when I go to see him now, but for a while there were frowns and downward glances. He's coming out of hospital soon, and my girlfriend's going in to have our child, and I so desperately want them to meet, my granddad and my kid.

I suppose my songs have always been about escape, and I sang a lot about death at the end of The Libertines and the beginning of Dirty Pretty Things. But maybe that's changing. The last song on my debut solo album, the last noise on the bar, is my baby's heartbeat. I sampled it during the twelve-week scan. Maybe now I'm trying to sing about life.

12/9/98

the 'Albion', of late, has
been subject to tempest
after tempest, in these
far flung and un-charted
corners of this dimension.
periods of calm to me
now, are nothing more
than omens of the ill
impending troubles. whether
this damage (inflicted by
the anarchy and selfishness
of some of those crewmen
aboard) can be sustained
for any length of time is
proving to be my cardinal
concern and in the remaining
hours, be they seconds or

Epilogue

The Longest Week of My Life

Let's rewind a year or two, back to when The Libertines were over and Dirty Pretty Things had gone. Love had withered and died on the vine and I'd broken up with my girlfriend. I was oblivious, and desensitized, not even able to drag on my martial arts whites and go and kick people. Was I in limbo or purgatory – was I waiting to be called upstairs or sent down to the boiler room in the cellar? At that point I didn't know, but whichever it was, it was well appointed, if dirty. There was drink, there were drugs and there were girls, and I'd come to in my kitchen and there'd be dishes piled waiting to be washed in greasy, grey water, pizza boxes stacked higher than the sink, rodents running around in the ruins. Everything that could be used as an ashtray was an ashtray: I lost count of the times I pulled at a cold cup of coffee or tea and felt the dirty remnants of ash in my mouth. Most nights I'd be surrounded by people I didn't recognize, strange laughter and music up the stairs, and I'd get paranoid and wonder who'd invited them. Usually, it was me; I'd be useless at keeping a

215

vampire at bay. People seemed glad to see me, but I couldn't for the life of me place them, which put me at a disadvantage. After a while that stopped mattering to me. I didn't even know what day it was; I could only guess the time by the light outside. Someone called my name, but it was no one I knew.

Somehow, I had to break the cycle of waking up, going to the pub, meeting strangers, inviting them back to my house, tearing days out of my diary, finally coming to, people prostrate everywhere, and checking my watch to see if the pub was open. Repeat to fade. Then, a moment of clarity in this smoke-filled madness: I decided to cap it all off, this misery and despair, by staying up for a whole week. I'd deprived myself of sleep before, three-day benders on a heady cocktail (isn't that what they say?) of whisky, lager and cocaine. For years it was my natural state but, for some reason, I hoped a week without sleep would draw a line under things and somehow let me start living again. I thought it was some kind of epiphany at the time, but in reality it was just skewed thinking from a man at the end of his tether. I was sick of being alone and I was sick of my lifestyle, so I opted to purge myself through excess, bleed myself dry to make things better. I wanted to get closer to my mortality, I was fed up with how pointless it all was, fed up with wrecking everything. Although a number of things had led me to this, in hindsight only one of them was important. I'd just met Edie, and I could tell even then that she would be worth it. It'll tell you a lot about my state of mind that I thought this was the only answer – although you should realize by now that I can't do things by halves (although these days I'm trying). I really didn't know what would happen, but for once I felt like I had an interesting point to make.

* * *

I was in Stockholm when it started, playing a solo show. It was early summer 2009, and the weekend before Glastonbury; I wasn't going to sleep until after it had finished. I applied some spurious science to my undertaking: any longer than a week and I'd probably run a serious risk of dying or not coming back, so seven days was the limit.

Drugs are hard to score in Stockholm and, believe me, I've tried. Luckily, I had some drug buddies in town and I knew they were on their way so after I came off stage I just stayed awake and sat around waiting for them to deliver. There were two acts on the festival bill that had caught my eye for completely different reasons: Mötley Crüe and Peter. I managed to see neither. I just gorged on drugs thinking, *This is it, what's the point of fucking sleeping at all?*

I don't remember much about getting home from Stockholm. There are fragments of being dazed by a news-stand in the airport, and the man behind the counter asking me if I wanted a newspaper or a magazine. Then, when I didn't answer, he asked me if I wanted help. I wanted to tell him that love wasn't the answer, for some reason, but waved him away instead. Then I stood by the giant window that looks out on to the runways, the jets beyond silently rising and falling in and out of the sky. I came to in London, in my flat, or that's how it seemed. There were no clean dishes, nothing to eat off, and the windows looked dirty, although I couldn't be sure if that was just me. I turned to my flatmate Mario and asked him if he thought so too, but he just shrugged and pushed at a pizza box with his foot. Lack of sleep and the cocaine were making me itchy, my mouth felt like it belonged to someone else and the skin around my eyes felt dense and rubbery. I hadn't shaved, I couldn't be sure I'd washed. I would, however, almost certainly have bet that it was Tuesday, a time that I'd identified in my strategic campaign planning as a danger point – a lull between Stockholm and Glastonbury that might threaten my endeavour to ride out a week awake. I knew I had to be in London until we could head west on Thursday morning, so I dragged Mario down to the pub and ordered a pint of lager and a Jameson's. Voices sounded a long way off and the light coming through the window was too bright, then the man we were waiting for came through the pub door, and with a nod I was up so quickly from behind our table I almost made the glasses tip over. Beer sloshed everywhere. The people at the next table gave me an admonishing look, but I was already away sampling the goods in the toilet cubicle, lining my pockets with tightly packed wraps of cocaine. I was on the dark side of the moon, on cloud nine, through the looking glass, past the wardrobe and out among the fields of Narnia. I was quite simply the cat in the hat.

Halfway home, my flatmate came panting down the hill. 'You left me sitting on my own in the pub,' he said. 'I finished your drinks.' It seemed like I hadn't seen him in ages. I hugged him and felt triumphant.

* * *

In the blink of an eye I was on the M4, reading road signs aloud, travelling to one of my favourite places in the world. It was early on Thursday morning – I knew this because I'd asked everyone in the car three or four times, just to check. No bands to be in, no shows to play, just a punter. My manager at the time was driving us and I had the window open to feel the air on my face. I was feeling good about things: it was one of the bursts of enthusiasm that usually lasted an hour, only to be replaced by a black cloud of despair, which was then followed by more sudden sunshine. I could best be described as acting erratically. I had organized us accommodation a while before, a tepee from a lady who just happened to be launching a lingerie company called Dirty Pretty Things. I said I was happy for her to use the name; she gave us a tepee in the field she was organizing in return. Led Zeppelin had the Riot House on Sunset when they wanted to let loose; I had a tent based on a classic Native American design somewhere near Pilton.

Glastonbury has always been close to my heart. I went to my first festival when I was one, the year Hawkwind were playing, I think, and Lemmy was still in the band. Back then, my parents were still together, and Glastonbury was the sort of place where my three-year-old sister could get lost without fear of harm. It really was all fields round there, not the tent city it's become. I visited again and again, and had one of my first real emancipating experiences there, when I was about twenty-one, around the time I was staying in Dalston with the ketamine-cooking French girls. Peter hadn't come with us, for some reason, but I drove down with two mates, dodged the patrols,

Bravo Two Zero-style, and crawled through the fence to the land of the free, soon losing myself in a rainbow pool of acid, crouching on the side of the moon and uniting a band of merry men with my Huxleyan visions, disciples I then led through the night, liberating things from stalls.

Back in the year 2009, though, back in the tepee towards the end of the longest week of my life, I was sitting with The View, who, like me, were attracted like moths to the flame of the idea of not going to sleep. I'd often come back that weekend and the place would be filled with different people. It was in all honesty, fucking mayhem, which suited my mood. I wanted the energy of others to keep me going on my journey, reasoning that, once I'd been through it all, I'd never have to do it all again. It was morning and The View looked slightly the worse for wear. They were having an argument over what looked like a piece of snot, something that even I couldn't see the point in doing. It was either a piece of snot or a raisin, which was probably the crux of the matter, but they couldn't decide, so they started fighting. I tried to get between them, but I couldn't tell if I was helping or not as I couldn't understand a word they were saying. There was a pause and then one of them, I forget which, grabbed the raisin (let's call it that for argument's sake) and ate it. There was a moment of blissful silence and them absolute mayhem as fighting broke out again. I sat outside and watched Saturday stirring as the shouting abated behind me.

Blur are my one abiding memory of that festival. They were amazing, and I was pleased, if only because Graham Coxon had been nice to me once along the way, when The Libertines had hardly really begun. I thought in my haze that Damon was being nice to the audience, but he'd told us to be cruel to ours. Everything felt like it was culminating in this, voices escaping the void, my history piling up around me and, for the first time Glastonbury felt like a lonely experience for me. I was lonely in myself because all I could see as I looked around was what other people had and I hadn't: families and love and a purpose. They looked like they were needed, and I didn't think I was.

I was standing in a field as night fell and we – my newfound fellow travellers and I – had found a bar. Hands were shaken, strangers hugged, someone sourced some more drugs and a cheer went up, then it was suddenly quiet and everyone stalked off into the darkness in different directions. I weaved around for a bit and then found myself sitting in the doorway of my own tepee, quite alone as the rain set in. I think that I'm in a film far too much at the best of times, but that really did feel like the anti-hero's dénouement and that I was destined to die alone. My bands had died, I had nothing left, I was past my sell-by date. My whole future seemed as if it might consist solely of that moment – all surface, no feeling, bouncing between orchestrated highs and chemical lows, roaming around a field near Glastonbury Tor with all the other has-beens trying to connect with a world they once knew. I hadn't slept in almost a week and, I realized, staying conscious was the extent of my quest, my life's ambitions at that point: how fucking noble. All I had to show for my past musical life was one big broken friendship, a lot of very faded memories and a free tepee at a festival that I'd managed to blag because someone wanted to sell knickers and bras with the same name as my old band. I clearly remember thinking that I wouldn't even have that currency next year. Nothing to show for it all, and nobody to share that nothing with. It was an end-of-the-road moment.

A few hours later, I'd bottomed out into something like clarity – perhaps, like Spinal Tap, too much fucking clarity – and began to wander through the VIP areas, full of rich girls partying in designer Wellingtons on daddy's coin and celebrities complaining they daren't go out into the crowds (which begs the question, why didn't you stay at home, you simpletons?). It's a strange world when you've got a pass to go literally anywhere even when you're not playing, so I just did a little tour, giving a cheery wave here and there like a country vicar on his rounds. I ended up sitting next to an English pop star, and, by then, I was experiencing a little lull. Consequently my grasp on my faculties loosened. Remember me on the *Soccer AM* sofa trying to explain to Noel Gallagher just what made him so great? Yep, just like that. I could barely speak, and little Miss Pop Star was absolutely disgusted with me. She looked like she'd never seen a puddle in her life, which was impressive considering we'd just been rained upon. She was bragging about taking helicopters to the shows she'd recently been playing in Europe, and I must have come to momentarily because it dawned on me that she was only touring large clubs and small theatres, so economically it made no sense. At that point, she got the right hump and was forced to explain to the gathered company that her travel tab was being paid by Mohamed Al Fayed. She was certainly keeping it real.

I didn't really fare any better with Jarvis Cocker, who was only a couple of tepees up from me (it really was quite the neighbourhood). He's one of the few people in the world – Brian Blessed being another – who makes me instantly star-struck, even though I'm almost certain that he doesn't like me (possibly due to a vague memory I have of chewing his ear off once, while off my face, when he was completely sober and probably with his kids). But not even that can deter the fan-boy face I adopt when he's anywhere near. I've met him a few times since Glastonbury and he's seemed . . . detached, shall we say, but I have such an artistic crush on him that it doesn't matter. After bothering Jarvis at his tepee for a while, I got into a fight with his old bass player, Steve Mackey, a fight that went on for hours, which is odd for a number of reasons. Firstly, I really like and admire Steve Mackey; secondly, we're friends; thirdly, ten minutes of kickboxing used to make me feel like I'd wrestled a bear, so how I made a fight last that long is one of life's great conundrums. It wasn't a real fight, more a hopeless tangle of bodies, though I did have my lip cut open a couple of hours later, when a friend of a friend came up at me out of the haze and smacked me in the face. There was a tussle, and blood in my mouth, but like so many cocaine moments there was a softness to its edges. My lip was swollen and then he was gone again. Drugs and a lack of sleep couched the moment for me and carried it all away. In retrospect, I think I was a little ragged by that point.

After the punch I found some sort of median between my erratic highs and lows, and I began to feel quite calm. My heart was no longer audible in my chest and, as I watched kids playing in the rain, I saw in them the different phases of my life as I grew up on those fields, coming back year after year, first with my mum, then with my mates, then with my bands. *I've done that*, I thought, as a kid went over in the mud and gurgled happily instead of breaking into tears. *I've been that boy in the hat and I've been her, the girl holding her dad's hand and looking up at him happily and I've been all these people and I've laughed that laugh and I've shouted what he's just shouted.* As I kept walking it all seemed to make sense, and it wasn't utterly morbid, it was kind of enlightening. With everything I saw, I kept thinking, *I don't need that any more. I've done that. I don't need to.*

The rest of the weekend consisted of getting wrecked with scallies from Manchester in their camping area, holding court in the tepee, completely off my rocker, and, later, calmly sitting with Emily Eavis taking it all in, every tier of life in the place – all the magic created by the motion of bodies and different worlds colliding, the weird and wonderful stalls, and people trying to make a difference – the soul of Glastonbury, I suppose. I even think I saw my mum, which isn't as far out as it sounds: she works there every year. It was uncomfortable seeing her in that state, but either she didn't notice or she pretended not to. It was probably best just to look away at that point. I don't think I went back to my tepee once in the final day or so; I figured that if I sat down in there it would literally be lights out, and, even if I had begun to come to terms with myself and the demise of both my bands, I was still determined to keep to the plan.

I was remarkably clear-headed as the sun came up on Monday morning, though Stockholm seemed like an age ago, another life, and

I couldn't quite remember if I'd started my seven days on Sunday or Monday. It didn't matter: if I made it through today then I'd done it. I could banish all the madness from my life and move on. That's how you talk and think when you've been doing cocaine and booze for a week – like a bad paperback. I thought about Danny from Supergrass, and when I dropped the pint into Sadie Frost's piano, as I waited for the car to come around and take us offsite. That was at the start of the band; that was when we were on the up and everything was still new and inexplicably exciting. I remembered sitting next to Danny on an old leather sofa, looking out of an open window on to one of Camden's most salubrious squares, trees making shadows of the streetlights. There was a girl standing near us, and I whispered to Danny that she was very pretty, but she looked like a fat Kate Moss. Then she turned around and it *was* Kate Moss, and she was pregnant. Why they let me stick around all summer I'll never know.

That thought took me all the way to Frome, where Danny and his family lived. There were three of us in the car: my manager, who'd been raging all weekend, me and Anthony Rossomando, who was sharing the journey back. We soon pulled away from the main road, full as it was with deranged looking kids clinging to their steering wheels, tops off and windows down, music that little bit too loud, off on to B roads and away from all that madness. The road got leafier by the mile, the views calmer, and then I experienced the softest of landings, sitting in Danny's garden to enjoy a family lunch, good food and a respite from all the recent insanity. Sitting outside digesting the first solids I could remember, I felt the warm air on my skin and

Anthony came and hugged me, then someone brought me a glass of wine. My manager had crumpled in a heap towards the bottom of the garden, and had rolled on to his back, blissfully asleep, his snoring the only sound for the next four hours. Suddenly, everything felt normal again, and I thought about Edie the cellist and, even if she wasn't really my girlfriend, how I still really missed her, but how that was somehow okay. The dread of being alone was fading, as if I'd purged – or beaten it – from my system.

* * *

The sky was black by the time we got back to London and I waved as the car pulled away. It was probably Tuesday by then, a new day just begun. From the high street down the long steep hill to my house there's a view of London that is extraordinary: you can see beyond the Gherkin and the West End, past the Millennium Dome and all the way down to Crystal Palace where the natural bowl that holds this city in place rises up again. I lit a cigarette and the smoke went straight to my head, then walked unsteadily down the hill. I let myself in and walked out to the kitchen where a mouse scurried through the darkness. I picked up a pizza box and looked for somewhere to put it, realized there was nowhere and threw it back on the floor. I'd clean tomorrow, I thought, and I think I actually meant it. I climbed the stairs and flopped down on my bed, the house quiet and still. Somewhere a car alarm was going off. I was tired, but I wasn't in despair. I didn't need to have strangers in my house any more. I didn't need to live life as a series of peaks and troughs. I had that choice. Later, I'd find a new manager who'd spot me playing as a surprise guest with Peter on YouTube; I'd find it in myself to write a new record, but alone this time; Edie the cellist would enter my life properly and save me in the process; I'd have a kid, and we'd reunite The Libertines . . . but I knew nothing of that then. I didn't know that happiness was waiting for me, I only knew that I had to give in, I had to let it come. I lay my head on the pillow and slept.